EVOLVE

WORKBOOK

Mari Vargo

3

CAMBRIDGE
UNIVERSITY PRESS

CAMBRIDGE
UNIVERSITY PRESS & ASSESSMENT

Shaftesbury Road, Cambridge CB2 8EA, United Kingdom

One Liberty Plaza, 20th Floor, New York, NY 10006, USA

477 Williamstown Road, Port Melbourne, VIC 3207, Australia

314–321, 3rd Floor, Plot 3, Splendor Forum, Jasola District Centre, New Delhi – 110025, India

103 Penang Road, #05–06/07, Visioncrest Commercial, Singapore 238467

Cambridge University Press & Assessment is a department of the University of Cambridge.

We share the University's mission to contribute to society through the pursuit of education, learning and research at the highest international levels of excellence.

www.cambridge.org
Information on this title: www.cambridge.org/9781108409001

First published 2019

20 19 18 17 16 15 14 13 12 11 10 9 8 7 6

Printed in Great Britain by CPI Group (UK) Ltd, Croydon CR0 4YY

A catalogue record for this publication is available from the British Library

ISBN 978-1-108-40527-0 Student's Book
ISBN 978-1-108-40507-2 Student's Book A
ISBN 978-1-108-40920-9 Student's Book B
ISBN 978-1-108-40528-7 Student's Book with Practice Extra
ISBN 978-1-108-40508-9 Student's Book with Practice Extra A
ISBN 978-1-108-40921-6 Student's Book with Practice Extra B
ISBN 978-1-108-40900-1 Workbook with Audio
ISBN 978-1-108-40872-1 Workbook with Audio A
ISBN 978-1-108-41193-6 Workbook with Audio B
ISBN 978-1-108-40517-1 Teacher's Edition with Test Generator
ISBN 978-1-108-41068-7 Presentation Plus
ISBN 978-1-108-41203-2 Class Audio CDs
ISBN 978-1-108-40793-9 Video Resource Book with DVD
ISBN 978-1-108-41447-0 Full Contact with DVD
ISBN 978-1-108-41154-7 Full Contact A with DVD
ISBN 978-1-108-41415-9 Full Contact B with DVD

Additional resources for this publication at www.cambridge.org/evolve

CONTENTS

UNIT 1 WHO WE ARE

1.1 WHAT'S YOUR PERSONALITY?

1 VOCABULARY: Describing personality

A **Read a woman's descriptions of three people she knows. Then check (✓) <u>three</u> words that describe each person.**

1 My friend Anna is always in a good mood and spends a lot of time with friends. She doesn't get upset about little problems like missing the bus or losing her keys. But she's usually about 30 minutes late when we get together because she can't find her keys!

☑ cheerful ☐ nervous ☐ easygoing ☐ sociable ☐ reliable

2 Marco is eight years older than me. He's my brother, but sometimes he's more like a parent. He gives me money when I need it for rent or food. He gave me a room in his house when I first started school. He even protected me from our neighbor's angry dog when I was little. He's great, but he doesn't always tell me the truth. I mean, he never tells me when he has a problem. He doesn't want me to worry.

☐ brave ☐ generous ☐ honest ☐ selfish ☐ helpful

3 My friend James is the smartest person I know. He reads one or two books a week. I don't see him very often because he's always at home reading or studying. When we get together, we have interesting conversations about science and politics. I like talking with him, but some people don't feel the same way because he always tells them when they say something that's wrong.

☐ easygoing ☐ intelligent ☐ nervous ☐ serious ☐ honest

B **Describe yourself. Use the personality words from exercise 1A.**

____

____

____

____

2 GRAMMAR: Information questions

A **Put the words in the correct order to write questions. Then match the questions with the answers.**

1 you / do / work / kind of / What / do / ? ___d___

What kind of work do you do?

2 you / Why / Japanese / are / learning / ? ______

______

3 teacher / your / Who's / Japanese / ? ______

______

4 do / in / Which / you / live / neighborhood / ? ______

______

5 is / next / When / class / your / ? ______

______

6 class / in / are / history / you / Whose / ? ______

______

a It's Professor Kubota.

b Professor King's class.

c It's at 2:00.

d I'm a nurse.

e I'm going to Japan this summer.

f I live near the university.

3 GRAMMAR AND VOCABULARY

A **Imagine a new student has just joined your class, and you want to find out about his or her personality. What questions can you ask? Complete the questions with your own ideas.**

1 What is the most ______?

2 Where do you love to ______?

3 How do you feel when ______?

4 When was the last time you ______?

5 Who do you spend ______?

6 Why ______?

B **Answer the questions from exercise 3A with true information.**

1 ______

2 ______

3 ______

4 ______

5 ______

6 ______

1.2 TRUE FRIENDS?

1 VOCABULARY: Giving personal information

A **Complete the sentences with the words and phrases in the box.**

am into	are married	are single	celebrate
live alone	live with my family	was born	was raised

1 I ______________ in the 1980s. My birthday is June 18, 1984.
2 I ______________ in a big city. I loved growing up in Hong Kong.
3 Both of my brothers ______________ . I don't have any sisters-in-law.
4 My best friend and I ______________ to two amazing men. Now our husbands are friends, too.
5 I ______________ . I can't have my own apartment until I get a job.
6 I think it's fun to ______________ . I can sing out loud and no one can hear me.
7 I ______________ video games. Sometimes I play them all night long.
8 I usually ______________ my birthday with my family. We usually go out to dinner and have cake at home.

2 GRAMMAR: Indirect questions

A **Complete the conversation with the questions and answers in the box.**

Do you know where she was born?
I want to find out what kinds of things she's into.
~~Can you tell me what movies she was in?~~
I wonder how old she is.
I wonder if she lives with her family.

A I'm reading about the actress Hailee Steinfeld. Do you like her?
B I don't know. [1]*Can you tell me what movies she was in?*
A She was in *The Edge of Seventeen* and *Pitch Perfect 2*.
B Oh, yeah. I like her. [2] ______________
A She was born in 1996, so she's the same age as you.
B [3] ______________
A I think she was born in California.
B [4] ______________
A I don't know. I think she lives alone. [5] ______________
B Well, we know she's into singing.
A Do you know if she's in a new movie?
B I don't know. Let's find out ...

B **Complete an indirect question for each answer. Include the correct punctuation – a period or a question mark. Remember: Do not use *do/does* in indirect questions.**

1 **A** Do you know ___how old he is?___
B He's 20 years old.

2 **A** Can you tell me ______
B He's into baseball.

3 **A** I wonder ______
B He was born in Pusan, South Korea.

4 **A** Do you know ______
B He was raised in Seoul.

5 **A** I'd like to know ______
B He lives with his family.

3 GRAMMAR AND VOCABULARY

A **Imagine you are having a conversation with a friend about a famous person. Complete the indirect questions. Then write responses to the questions. You can make up information about the famous person or check on the internet.**

Choose the famous person:

______

Find out how old the person is.

A Do you know [1] ___when___ he/she [2] ______?
B ______

Ask where the person lived as a child.

A I wonder [3] ______ he/she [4] ______.
B ______

Find out if the person is single or married.

A I'd like to know [5] ______ he/she [6] ______.
B ______

1.3 NICE TALKING TO YOU

1 FUNCTIONAL LANGUAGE: Making introductions, saying how you know someone, and ending a conversation

A **Put each sentence in the correct place in the chart.**

I work with Tony.	I'm Sonia.
~~This is Maria, my wife.~~	It was nice talking to you.
It was really nice to meet you.	How do you know Ivan?

Introductions	Saying how you know someone	Ending a conversation
This is Maria, my wife.		

B **Complete the conversation using sentences from exercise 1A. You do not need to use all of the sentences.**

A Hi! [1] ______________________ .

B Nice to meet you. So, [2] ______________________ ?

A Well, we worked together when we were in college.

B Cool. Oh wow, it's getting late. [3] ______________________ .

A It was good talking to you, too.

2 REAL-WORLD STRATEGY: Meeting someone you've heard about

A **Put the conversations in order.**

Conversation 1

It's nice to meet you, Brian. I've heard good things about you. ____

Hello. I'm Andy. I work with Tina. ____

Oh, that's nice. ____

Hi, Andy. I'm Brian. I'm Tina's brother. ____

Conversation 2

Hi, Ken. I'm Luis. It's nice to meet you. I've heard a lot about you. ____

Yes, only good things! ____

Hi, I'm Ken. I'm Tina's husband. ____

Good things, I hope! ____

3 FUNCTIONAL LANGUAGE AND REAL-WORLD STRATEGY

A **Read the information. Then complete the conversations with the correct words and phrases in the box.**

Conversation 1

Daniel is Heather's husband.

Heather and Tom are in school together.

I've heard good things about you!	in my English class	~~my husband~~	Oh, that's nice.

Heather Hi, Tom. This is Daniel, 1 ___my husband___ . Daniel, this is Tom. He is 2 ________ .

Daniel Hi, Tom. It's great to meet you. 3 ________

Tom 4 ________ I've heard good things about you, too!

Conversation 2

Vincent is Laurie's brother. Carlo works with Vincent.

Julia is Carlo's wife. Laurie is married to Sam.

husband	wife	Good things I hope!
work with	sister	I've heard a lot about you!

Carlo Hi, I'm Carlo. I 5 ________ Vincent. How do you know him?

Laurie Hi, Carlo. I'm Laurie, Vincent's 6 ________ .

Carlo 7 ________

Laurie 8 ________

Carlo Yes, only good things! This is my 9 ________ , Julia.

Laurie Hi, Julia. It's so nice to meet you. This is my 10 ________ , Sam.

B **Now imagine you are at a party with a friend, and you see a classmate. Introduce them. Have them say that they've heard about each other. Then end the conversation.**

You Hi, ________ ! How nice to see you here! This is my friend, ________ .

Friend ________ .

Classmate Hi, ________ . ________

Friend ________

Classmate ________

Friend ________

Classmate ________

You ________

1.4 WE'RE FAMILY!

1 READING

A **READ FOR DETAIL** **Read the email. Then read the statements and check (✓) *True, False,* or *Not given*.**

To: ericanyc@cup.org
From: ditamx@cup.org
Subject: Info about Boston

Hi Erica,

My name is Dita. I live in Mexico City. You work with my sister, Belen, in New York. She gave me your email address. I hope that's OK. I'm writing because I want to go to Boston, Massachusetts, next summer, and I'd like to find out more about it. Belen told me that you were raised in Boston. Can you tell me a little bit about the city?

I'm wondering what the weather is like in Boston in the summer. I'd also like to find out how much money I need. Do you know how much an apartment in the city costs? My friend Marta wants to come, too. She wants to live with me, so we need a two-bedroom apartment.

Marta and I are both into music. Do you know if there are any good places to listen to music? Can you tell me if there are big concert halls in Boston? What else can we do there?

Hope to hear from you soon.

Dita

	True	False	Not given
1 Dita lives in New York.	☐	☑	☐
2 Belen works in New York.	☐	☐	☐
3 Erica was born in Boston.	☐	☐	☐
4 Dita wants to go to Boston.	☐	☐	☐
5 Belen goes to school with Erica.	☐	☐	☐
6 Dita works at an office in Mexico City.	☐	☐	☐

2 LISTENING

A 1.01 **Listen to the conversation and circle the correct answers.**

1 Erica is talking to ________________ .
  a Dita (b) Belen c Marta

2 Erica ________________ Dita's email.
  a read b answered c didn't get

3 Erica says that Boston is ________________ .
  a an expensive city b a safe city c a busy place

4 Boston has a lot of ________________ .
  a sports teams b rain c colleges

3 WRITING

A **Imagine Dita is asking you about your city. Reply to her email. Write paragraphs about your city.**

Hi, Dita.

It was great to hear from you. ______________________________

CHECK AND REVIEW

Read the statements. Can you do these things?

UNIT 1	Mark the boxes. ☑ I can do it. ? I am not sure. **I can …**	If you are not sure, go back to these pages in the Student's Book.
VOCABULARY	☐ **use adjectives to describe personality.** ☐ **use words to give personal information.**	page 2 page 4
GRAMMAR	☐ **ask information questions.** ☐ **use indirect questions.**	page 3 page 5
FUNCTIONAL LANGUAGE	☐ **make introductions and say how you know someone.** ☐ **meet someone you've heard about.**	page 6 page 7
SKILLS	☐ **use paragraphs in an email.** ☐ **use different opening and closing sentences in an email.**	page 9 page 9

UNIT 2 SO MUCH STUFF

2.1 MY GARAGE

1 VOCABULARY: Describing possessions

A **Find 11 more vocabulary words or phrases in the word search.**

M	O	D	C	G	M	N	I	D	L	V	U	A	I	Z
B	(U	S	E	F	U	L)	U	G	O	T	M	N	N	P
Y	B	O	N	W	R	F	P	C	V	B	X	L	G	M
T	R	S	A	Y	C	N	S	I	C	O	M	M	O	N
U	A	G	M	O	D	E	R	N	C	U	P	T	O	K
D	N	F	D	D	A	L	O	I	F	G	Z	U	D	T
U	D	O	T	T	M	N	M	A	B	D	Y	S	C	G
S	N	P	I	X	A	D	G	D	M	L	N	E	O	U
C	E	V	N	A	G	C	U	S	O	O	T	L	N	L
P	W	A	C	I	E	O	U	T	D	A	T	E	D	A
X	O	M	F	B	D	L	V	Z	A	F	C	S	I	C
U	P	T	G	M	H	F	A	N	C	Y	U	S	T	U
S	P	E	C	I	A	L	E	N	K	D	S	M	I	C
E	C	R	D	R	A	H	C	I	U	B	P	G	O	V
D	B	T	O	D	U	M	F	L	P	L	A	I	N	I

brand new
common
damaged
fancy
in good condition
modern
outdated
plain
special
useless
~~useful~~
used

B **Complete the sentences with the words and phrases in the box.**

brand new | in good condition | outdated | special | useless

1 My comic books might be worth a lot of money some day, so I keep them in a ______________ box.
2 This sweater is ______________. I just bought it yesterday.
3 I need a new phone. Mine is really ______________.
4 Don't throw that bike away. It's still ______________. You can sell it.
5 I don't know why I still have this broken printer. It's ______________.

2 GRAMMAR: Present perfect with *ever, never, for,* and *since*

A **Circle *ever, never, for,* or *since* to complete each sentence.**

1 I've had this phone *ever / never / (for) / since* three years.
2 Have you known Mike *ever / never / for / since* a long time?
3 These old computer games have *ever / never / for / since* worked!
4 You haven't been here *ever / never / for / since* last year.
5 Have your friends *ever / never / for / since* given you something really special?
6 We've ridden the same bikes *ever / never / for / since* years.
7 He's lived here *ever / never / for / since* 2015.

B **Complete the conversations. Use the present perfect forms of the verbs in parentheses ( ). Use *for* or *since* in the answers.**

1 **A** How long ___have___ you ___had___ these shoes? (have)
B I ______ them ______ a long time. (have)

2 **A** ______ you ever ______ this guitar? (play)
B Yes, I ______ guitar lessons ______ I was ten years old. (take)

3 **A** How long ______ this television ______ damaged? (be)
B It ______ damaged ______ last year. (be)

4 **A** ______ you ______ this bike recently? (use)
B No, I ______ it ______ about a year. (use)

5 **A** How long ______ your brother ______ this car? (have)
B He ______ it ______ he finished college. (own)

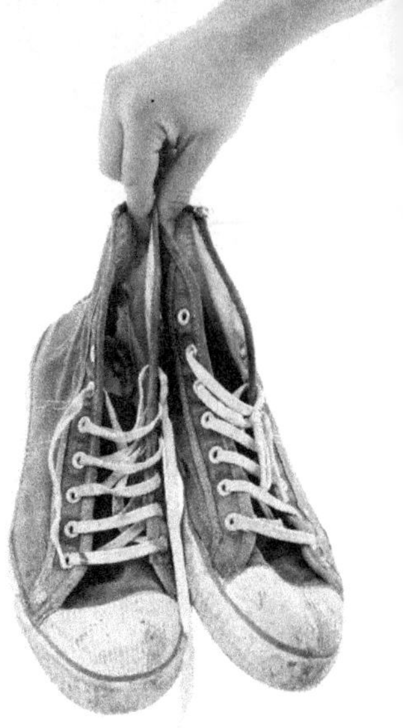

3 GRAMMAR AND VOCABULARY

A **Complete the chart with your own ideas. Write two more phrases for each verb.**

have	ride	play
have shoes	ride a bike	play computer games
own	**watch**	**collect**
own souvenirs	watch a DVD	collect ______

B **Write questions with *Have you ever* and phrases from the chart in exercise 3A.**

1 Have you ever played computer games?
2 ______
3 ______
4 ______
5 ______
6 ______

C **Write answers to the questions from exercise 3B. Use *never*, *for*, or *since* and add details.**

1 I haven't played computer games since I was in first grade.
2 ______
3 ______
4 ______
5 ______
6 ______

2.2 SO MANY FEATURES

1 VOCABULARY: Tech features

A **Match the two parts of the sentences to complete the definitions.**

1 A **device** is ______
2 If you **delete** something, ______
3 A **folder** is ______
4 Your **home screen** is ______
5 A **model** of something is ______
6 If you **set** something **up**, ______
7 The **storage** on a computer is ______
8 If you **sync** a phone to a computer, ______
9 If you **try** something, ______
10 If something **works**, ______

a you make it ready to use.
b you match the two things so they have the same information.
c you erase or remove it from a computer.
d one type of that thing, such as a phone or a car.
e it functions well, or it is successful.
f the screen you see when you start using your phone or computer.
g something you use for doing a special job.
h you use it for the first time to see what it is like.
i a place on a computer or phone where you organize files and apps.
j the space where a computer saves everything, including photos, music, and apps.

2 GRAMMAR: Present perfect with *already* and *yet*

A **Complete each sentence with *already* or *yet*.**

1 Have you set up your new laptop ______ ?
2 I haven't finished my homework ______ .
3 Stella has ______ deleted the email.
4 Lee hasn't called me ______ .
5 We've ______ bought new phones.

B **Find one mistake in each sentence. Then rewrite the sentence correctly.**

1 She's taken already that computer class.

______

2 Have yet you used your new laptop?

______

3 We haven't seen the new model already.

______

4 He's set up already his phone.

______

5 I've downloaded that song yet, but I'm going to later.

______

3 GRAMMAR AND VOCABULARY

A **Read Mark's and Tina's to-do lists. What things have they finished? What do they still have to do? Write sentences using the present perfect with *already* or *yet*.**

Mark's To-Do List

- ✓ set up my new phone
- sync all my devices
- ✓ delete folders on my home screen
- ✓ try my new apps
- buy more storage for my computer

Tina's To-Do List

- ✓ set up my new phone
- sync all my devices
- ✓ delete folders on my home screen
- change the picture on my home screen
- ✓ delete old emails

1 They've already set up their new phones.
2 They ______
3 They ______
4 Mark ______
5 Tina ______
6 Mark ______
7 Tina ______

B **Write your to-do list from yesterday. Check (✓) two things you've already done. Leave one thing you haven't done yet.**

My To-Do List

☐ ______

☐ ______

☐ ______

C **Write sentences about your notes in exercise 3B. Use *already* and *yet*.**

1 ______
2 ______
3 ______

2.3 GUESS WHAT?

1 FUNCTIONAL LANGUAGE: Introducing topics, changing the subject, and staying on track

A **Complete the conversation with the correct words and phrases.**

anyway by the way guess what oh, before I forget ~~you know~~

A It's so good to see you, Ed!
B Yeah, I haven't seen you in a long time, Misha! What's new?
A Well, [1] _____you know_____ I was looking for a bigger apartment because I have so much stuff.
B Yes, I remember. Did you move?
A Not yet, but [2] __________ ? My building manager quit last month, and I'm the new manager!
B Congratulations! I hope you're a nice apartment manager!
A Of course! [3] __________ , I have to work more now, but I can have a bigger apartment.
B I'm so happy for you. [4] __________ , my sister asked me to say "hello" to you.
A That's nice. Tell her I said, "hi," too. How is she?
B She's great. [5] __________ , I saw your brother at school last week. He's in my English class.
A Really? I didn't know that!

2 REAL-WORLD STRATEGY: Using short questions to show interest

A **Put the conversation in order.**

A I went to Los Angeles last weekend with my sister. ___1___
B She did? What did she buy? _____
B You are? Why do you want to go back? _____
A Yeah, we had a great time, but it's really expensive there. _____
A Well, we went shopping. My sister bought a lot of stuff. _____
A My sister wants to return all her dresses and shoes! _____
A A few dresses and five pairs of shoes. We're planning to go back next month. _____
B Really? Did you have fun? _____
B It is? What did you do that cost so much money? _____

3 FUNCTIONAL LANGUAGE AND REAL-WORLD STRATEGY

A **Find and correct <u>three</u> errors in each conversation.**

Conversation 1

A You know I collect old toy cars, right?
B You did? I didn't know that.
A Yeah, I do, and guess where? I found a box full of toy cars in my uncle's garage!
B You were? Wow, that's great!
A I know, and they're in really good condition, too.

Conversation 2

A My roommate and I cleaned our apartment last weekend, and we gave away a bunch of stuff.
B You are? What did you give away?
A Mostly clothes and books. By the was, I found your sweater. You left it at my house.
B I was? When did I leave it there?
A I think you left it last week. I can bring it to class tomorrow.
B Thanks.

B **Complete the conversation with your own ideas. Use phrases to introduce new topics, change the subject, and stay on track. Include short questions to show interest.**

A So, you know I like to go to garage sales.
B Yeah, you always find a lot of really cool old stuff.
A That's right. Well, [1] ________________ ? I found [2] ________________ yesterday!
B [3] ________________ ? Where did you find it?
A It was [4] ________________ .
B [5] ________________ ? How much did you pay for it?
A Kind of a lot. The guy wanted [6] ________________ for it.
B Wow! How much do you think it's actually worth?
A It's worth about [7] ________________ ! Oh, sorry, my phone is ringing.
B That's OK.
A Hmm … It's a wrong number. [8] ________________ , isn't that amazing?
B Yeah, it is. By the way, I want to go with you next time!
A Of course! Why don't you come with me on Sunday?

2.4 IT'S USELESS, RIGHT?

1 LISTENING

A 2.01 LISTEN FOR DETAIL **Listen to the conversation. Read each statement and write *T* (true) or *F* (false).**

1 James is at Kevin's house. ____
2 Kevin's dad collected a lot of different things. ____
3 Kevin's dad wants Kevin to organize everything and give it away. ____
4 James can help Kevin because he isn't busy today. ____
5 James agrees that Kevin should give everything away. ____

B 2.01 **Listen to the conversation again. Circle the correct answers.**

1 What did Kevin's dad collect?
a coins, stamps, and watches **b** books, coins, and baseball cards **c** watches and chairs
2 What does Kevin have to do?
a sell everything online **b** put everything in the garage **c** count everything
3 What is worth $500?
a a coin **b** a book **c** a baseball card
4 How does James find the price?
a He looks in a book. **b** He looks online. **c** He asks Kevin's dad.

2 READING

A **Read Kevin's notes for his first ad. Then circle the best ad for this item.**

baseball card	2001
Ichiro Suzuki	signed on front
Seattle Mariners	$400
Good condition	

a I'm selling a baseball card. It is in good condition and is signed on the front. Suzuki played for the Seattle Mariners.

b Are you looking for an Ichiro Suzuki baseball card? I have one. It's from 2001, and I'm asking $400 for it.

c This Ichiro Suzuki baseball card is in good condition. It is from 2001 and has Suzuki's signature on the front. $400

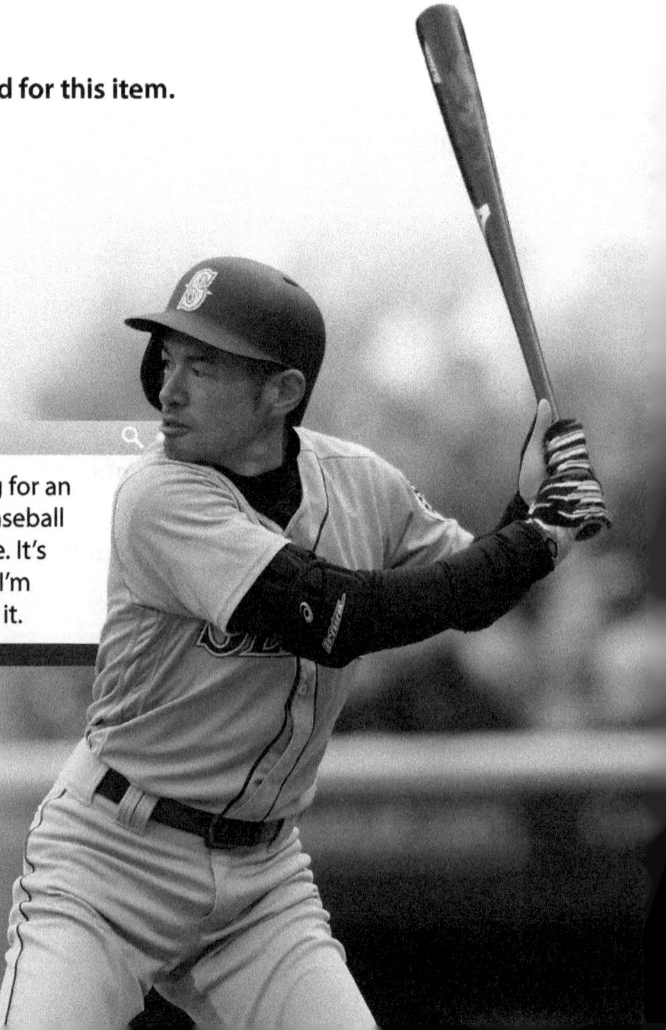

3 WRITING

A **Think of something that you want to sell. What does the item look like? Make notes and suggest a price.**

Condition: ______________________

Age: ______________________

Color: ______________________

Other: ______________________

Price: ______________________

B **Use the information from exercise 3A to write an ad for your item. Use *one* and *ones* to avoid repetition.**

CHECK AND REVIEW

Read the statements. Can you do these things?

UNIT 2	Mark the boxes. ☑ I can do it. [?] I am not sure. **I can …**	If you are not sure, go back to these pages in the Student's Book.
VOCABULARY	☐ **describe possessions.** ☐ **talk about tech features.**	page 12 page 14
GRAMMAR	☐ **use the present perfect with *ever, never, for,* and *since*.** ☐ **use the present perfect with *already* and *yet*.**	page 13 page 15
FUNCTIONAL LANGUAGE	☐ **introduce topics, change the subject, and stay on track.** ☐ **use short questions to show interest.**	page 16 page 17
SKILLS	☐ **write an ad for something I want to sell.** ☐ **use *one* and *ones* to avoid repetition.**	page 19 page 19

UNIT 3 SMART MOVES

3.1 INS AND OUTS

1 VOCABULARY: City features

A **Put the words in the correct places in the chart.**

bridge	clinic	embassy	ferry	fire station	highway
hostel	monument	parking lot	sidewalk	sculpture	tunnel

Buildings where people work	Things related to transportation	Other

2 GRAMMAR: Articles

A **Match each sentence with the correct rule.**

1 He's at the airport. ______
2 I don't like milk. ______
3 My brother is a doctor. ______

a Don't use an article when you talk about something in general.
b Use *a*/*an* to talk about singular nouns.
c Use *the* with something your listener already knows about.

B **Complete the sentences with the words and phrases in the box. Add *a*, *an*, or *the* where necessary.**

bank	grocery store	Madrid	Pine Street	tallest building	trains

1 I live in ______________, but I didn't grow up in the city.
2 Is there ______________ near here? I need to get some money.
3 Buses are slower than ______________.
4 I think my friend lives on ______________.
5 That's ______________ in town – it has 40 floors.
6 Can you please get some milk at ______________?

C **Circle *a, an, the,* or Ø (no article).**

1 We saw *a* / *an* / *the* / Ø beautiful monument today. I don't know what it's called.
2 I think *a* / *an* / *the* / Ø Tokyo is the most exciting city in the world.
3 I'm looking for *a* / *an* / *the* / Ø apartment downtown.
4 We're not far from *a* / *an* / *the* / Ø hotel. You can go get a jacket from your room.
5 Close *a* / *an* / *the* / Ø door. It's cold.
6 *A* / *An* / *The* / Ø last train leaves at midnight.
7 *A* / *An* / *The* / Ø best shops are on *a* / *an* / *the* / Ø Jones Street.
8 Have you ever been to *a* / *an* / *the* / Ø Kings Park in *a* / *an* / *the* / Ø Australia?

3 GRAMMAR AND VOCABULARY

A **Complete each question with a noun or noun phrase in the box and the correct article (or no article).**

bridges	clinic	hostels	monuments	most beautiful sculpture	parking lot

1 What is ______________________ in your city? Where is it? Who is the artist?
2 If you're sick, is there ______________________ nearby that you can go to?
3 Are there any ______________________ or cheap hotels in your city where travelers can stay?
4 Are there any ______________________ in town? Are they for driving on or for walking on?
5 Where can we leave our car? Is there ______________________ by the movie theater?
6 Does your city have any ______________________ or other landmarks? What are they for?

B **Now answer the questions in exercise 3A about your city.**

1 ______________________
2 ______________________
3 ______________________
4 ______________________
5 ______________________
6 ______________________

3.2 A MAP LIKE SPAGHETTI

1 VOCABULARY: Public transportation

A **Unscramble the letters to make words related to public transportation.**

1 arfe ______
2 lein ______
3 oobk ______
4 otuer ______
5 recdit ______
6 rrivlaa ______
7 maltinre ______
8 duchslee ______
9 uparreetd ______
10 otnrreesavi ______

B **Complete the travel agent's web page with words from exercise 1A. You do not need four of the words.**

Are you ready for a vacation? We can help you [1] ______ your flight, make a hotel [2] ______, and even come up with a daily [3] ______ of activities! We help you save money by offering the lowest [4] ______ – and we always find the most convenient [5] ______ to get you to and from your destination. Most of our flights are [6] ______, so you can sit back, relax, and get straight to your dream vacation!

2 GRAMMAR: Modals for advice

A **Put the conversation in the correct order.**

A When should we book them? ___
B I'd book tickets online. ___
A Would you take a bus to the city? 1
A OK. Thanks. ___
B I'd take the 9:00 train. ___
A Which train would you take? ___
B No, I wouldn't. I'd take a train. ___
A How can we book our tickets? ___
B You could book them right now. Here, use my phone. ___

B **Complete the conversations with modals for advice and the verbs in parentheses ( ). Different answers are possible.**

1 **A** You [1] *could take* a bus. (take)
  B Which bus [2] ________ I [3] ________ ? (take)
  A Well, I usually take the cross-town express bus.

2 **A** You [4] ________ by ferry. (go)
  B OK. How [5] ________ I [6] ________ my ticket? (book)
  A Just buy a ticket at the terminal.

3 **A** You and your friend [7] ________ to the airport too late. (not / get)
  B When [8] ________ we [9] ________ ? (leave)
  A At least three hours before your flight.

4 **A** Which train [10] ________ we [11] ________ to the park? (take)
  B You [12] ________ to the park. It's not far. (walk)

3 GRAMMAR AND VOCABULARY

A **Complete the instructions with words in the box and modals for advice.**

arrival	direct	fare	line	schedule	terminal

From: Monica Martin
To: Sarah Jong
Subject: How to get to my place

Hey, Sarah!

I'm so glad that you're coming to visit me next month. I know it's your first time flying, so here are some tips:

First, you [1] ________ book a [2] ________ flight so you don't have to stop anywhere on the way. I [3] ________ get a flight with an early [4] ________ because I have to work until 5:00. You [5] ________ take a taxi here, but I [6] ________ take the train. A train ticket is much cheaper than a taxi [7] ________ . You can get to the train station from any [8] ________ in the airport. You [9] ________ take the L, M, or N [10] ________ . You [11] ________ check the train [12] ________ to see what time the trains leave and pick the best one. You [13] ________ get off the train at the 9th Street or 10th Street station. My apartment is between the two stations.

I can't wait to see you!

xo,

Monica

3.3 UP AND DOWN

1 FUNCTIONAL LANGUAGE: Asking for and giving directions

A **Match the sentence halves.**

1 Can you tell me how	______	a	meeting room 22 is on?
2 Which way	______	b	the first hallway.
3 Do you know which floor	______	c	to get to the elevator?
4 How do I	______	d	in the lobby.
5 It's on	______	e	is on your right.
6 Go down	______	f	get to the main entrance?
7 Room 332	______	g	is room 332?
8 It's downstairs	______	h	the second floor.

2 REAL-WORLD STRATEGY: Repeating details to show you understand

A **Complete the conversations. Repeat details to show you understand.**

1 **A** Where's the closest restroom?
  B ______________________________? It's down the hall on your right.
2 **A** Excuse me. Can you tell me how to get to the train station downtown?
  B ______________________________? Sure, just go down Stark Avenue and it's on the left.
3 **A** I'm really hungry. Where's the cafeteria?
  B ______________________________? It's in building B.
4 **A** Which way is the computer lab that has printers in it?
  B ______________________________? It's upstairs on the third floor.
5 **A** Do you know which floor the main office is on?
  B ______________________________? It's downstairs on the first floor.

3 FUNCTIONAL LANGUAGE AND REAL-WORLD STRATEGY

A **Imagine you work at your favorite restaurant or café. Complete the customers' questions using the phrases in the box. Give answers. Then write responses. Remember to repeat details to show you understand.**

do I get to	way is the	you tell me where

Conversation 1

A Excuse me, which [1] ______________________ *nearest ATM?*

B Oh, just go out the front door and [2] ______________________. But did you know you can pay with a credit card here?

A [3] ______________________

Conversation 2

A Can you help me? How [4] ______________________ *the bathroom?*

B Sure. It's [5] ______________________. Do you see the sign that says "restrooms"?

A [6] ______________________

Conversation 3

A Sorry, but can [7] ______________________ the coat closet is? I'd like to hang up my jacket.

B Yes, it's [8] ______________________. Wow, it's really raining out there! Would you like me to take your umbrella, too?

A [9] ______________________

B **Complete the questions about your home. Use the phrases in the box and the instructions in parentheses ( ). The phrases will be used more than once. Then answer the questions so they are true for you. Repeat details to show you understand.**

Can you tell me how to get to	How do I get to	Which way is

1 A ______________________
the kitchen? (from your living room)
B ______________________

2 A ______________________
the front door? (from your living room)
B ______________________

3 A ______________________
the bathroom? (from your kitchen)
B ______________________

4 A ______________________
the bedroom? (from the bathroom)
B ______________________

5 A ______________________
the living room? (from the bedroom)
B ______________________

3.4 MAYBE YOU CAN HELP!

1 READING

A **READ FOR DETAIL** **Read the ad. Then answer the questions.**

The 25th Annual Cross-City 10K Race is happening on May 27 – join the race or volunteer!

› RUN
The race route will take runners through the whole city. The race starts at the ferry terminal and ends at the soccer field in Miller Park. Sign up for the race online. The deadline to sign up is May 15. Click here to sign up.

› WATCH
Stand along the race route and cheer the runners on. After the race, stay and enjoy free food and drinks and a concert in the park. Click here to see the concert schedule.

› VOLUNTEER
Several of our runners are coming from out of town. A couple of days before the race, we need volunteers to meet them at the airport or the train station and tell them which buses or trains to take to get to their hotels. These volunteers will also give runners race information, schedules, and directions to the race's starting line. On race day, volunteers will stand on the race route and hand out water to all of the runners.

Volunteers should have a lot of energy, enjoy meeting new people, and know how to get around the city. Click here to volunteer.

1 What is the ad about?

____

2 What are three things that volunteers will have to do?

____

3 What three characteristics should volunteers have?

____

2 LISTENING

A 3.01 **Listen to the conversation. Circle the correct answers to the questions.**

1 What does Anna want to do?
   a run   b volunteer
2 What does Robin want to do?
   a run   b volunteer
3 Why does Anna know the city well?
   a She's lived there for a long time.   b She goes to school in the city.
4 Why doesn't Robin know the city well?
   a She doesn't go out very much.   b She moved there a few months ago.
5 Has Robin ever run in a race?
   a yes   b no

3 WRITING

A **Imagine you want to be a volunteer for the race in exercise 1A. Complete the application. Then check your punctuation and grammar.**

1 Why do you want to be a volunteer?

___

2 Have you ever volunteered for anything before?

___

3 Why do you think you would be a good volunteer?

___

4 Do you like meeting new people? Why or why not?

___

5 Do you know the city well? Write directions from one place in the city to another place.

___

CHECK AND REVIEW

Read the statements. Can you do these things?

UNIT 3	Mark the boxes. ☑ I can do it. [?] I am not sure. **I can …**	If you are not sure, go back to these pages in the Student's Book.
VOCABULARY	☐ **identify different features in my city.** ☐ **talk about traveling and using public transportation.**	page 22 page 24
GRAMMAR	☐ **use articles correctly.** ☐ **use modals to give advice.**	page 23 page 25
FUNCTIONAL LANGUAGE	☐ **ask for and give directions.** ☐ **repeat details to show I understand.**	page 26 page 27
SKILLS	☐ **complete an application.** ☐ **check my own writing for accuracy and correct use of grammar and punctuation.**	page 29 page 29

UNIT 4 THINK FIRST

4.1 HERO OR ZERO?

1 VOCABULARY: Describing opinions and reactions

A **Complete the sentences with the words in the box. Add the correct ending (*-ed* or *-ing*) to each word.**

amuse	annoy	disappoint	embarrass
fascinate	frighten	shock	surprise

1 It's so ___annoying___ when people park in my parking space!
2 The movie was kind of funny. I was ______, but I didn't really laugh out loud.
3 I forgot my wallet today, so I couldn't pay for my lunch. I had to borrow money from a co-worker. It was really ______ .
4 I'm ______ that I didn't get the job. I really wanted it.
5 I couldn't believe that I won a new car. I was ______ !
6 This book had a ______ ending. I expected it to end differently.
7 Tom loves to read about space exploration. He thinks it's ______ .
8 My sister never watches scary movies. She gets too ______ .

2 GRAMMAR: *be going to* and *will* for predictions

A **Put the words in the correct order to write predictions.**

1 get / work / He / won't / to / time / on / .
He won't get to work on time.
2 she's / going / us / think / to / I / don't / with / come / .
______
3 to / great / going / We're / time / have / a / .
______
4 well / this / I'll / do / school / year / in / .
______
5 and / late / Mark / dinner / I / be / for / will / .
______
6 like / idea / He's / to / this / going / not / .
______

B **Rewrite the sentences from exercise 2A. Change *be going to* to *will* and *will* to *be going to*.**

1 He's not going to get to work on time.
2 ______
3 ______
4 ______
5 ______
6 ______

3 GRAMMAR AND VOCABULARY

A **Complete the predictions with the correct form of the phrases in parentheses ( ) and the words in the box.**

amused	annoyed	disappointed	frightened	surprising

1 My son is scared of storms, and it is going to thunder tonight. (be going to / thunder) I hope he doesn't feel too ______.
2 My mom ______ this funny photo. (will / love) She'll be so ______!
3 Do you think your friends ______ really sad you can't go to the show? (be going to / be) I hope they aren't too ______.
4 My travel app says the bus ______ 15 minutes late this morning. (will / arrive) I'm so ______!
5 I don't think my boss ______ that I dyed my hair a different color. (will / care) Things like that aren't usually very ______ to her.

B **Complete the predictions with your own ideas. Use *will* or *be going to*.**

1 My parents are going to be surprised when I come home for my mother's birthday.
2 My ______ annoyed when ______.
3 I don't think my ______ shocked when ______.
4 It ______ frightening when ______.
5 I think it ______ disappointing when ______.
6 It ______ amusing when ______.

4.2 A PERUVIAN ADVENTURE

1 VOCABULARY: Making decisions and plans

A **Match the sentence halves.**

1 Let's arrange d
2 Don't forget ____
3 I'm going to meet up ____
4 Did you deal with ____
5 Can you let them know ____

a to bring your driver's license on the trip.
b the hotel reservations?
c that we're going to be late?
d a coffee date this week.
e with some friends for dinner tonight.

B **Complete the sentences with the phrases in the box.**

Can you check	~~How can I get in touch~~	I have to think about this
Let's look into	Please remind me	

1 How can I get in touch with you when you're on your trip?
2 ____ the weather on your phone?
3 ____ to buy our plane tickets tonight.
4 ____ before I make a decision.
5 ____ staying at a hotel near the beach.

2 GRAMMAR: *will* for sudden decisions; present continuous for future plans

A **Choose the correct verb form to complete each question. Then answer the questions.**

1 A What *will you do* / *are you doing* this weekend?
B I'm driving to the beach with my family.
2 A *Will you leave* / *Are you leaving* for your flight this afternoon?
B ____
3 A Someone is at the door. *Will you see* / *Are you seeing* who it is?
B ____
4 A *Will you take* / *Are you taking* a vacation in December?
B ____
5 A It's too late for your parents to call now. *Will they call* / *Are they calling* tomorrow?
B ____
6 A I don't want to cook tonight. *Will you buy* / *Are you buying* something for dinner on your way home?
B ____
7 A It's the twins' birthday on Friday. *Will they have* / *Are they having* a dinner party?
B ____

3 GRAMMAR AND VOCABULARY

A **Write answers to the questions with the words in parentheses ( ) and your own ideas. Write four sentences with *will* and four sentences with the present continuous.**

1 **A** What are you doing this weekend?
  B (meet up) *I'm meeting up with John at the park on Saturday.*
2 **A** Are we getting close to the airport?
  B (check) ______
3 **A** I think we're going to be about ten minutes late. Sandra must be wondering where we are.
  B (let Sandra know) ______
4 **A** Have you seen Kevin lately?
  B (get in touch) ______
5 **A** Have you made hotel reservations yet?
  B (deal with) ______
6 **A** I hope I don't forget to pack all my chargers.
  B (remind) ______
7 **A** When can I talk to your boss about a job?
  B (arrange) ______
8 **A** Do you want to go to the movies Friday night?
  B (think about) ______
9 **A** Do you know where you're going for your vacation?
  B (look into) ______

4.3 A DRIVING TEST

1 FUNCTIONAL LANGUAGE: Offering and responding to reassurance

A **Complete the conversations with the sentences in the box.**

I hope so.
I really appreciate it.
There's no need to worry.
He'll be fine.
Thanks, but I feel so bad.
~~It's no problem.~~
Don't worry about the clothes.

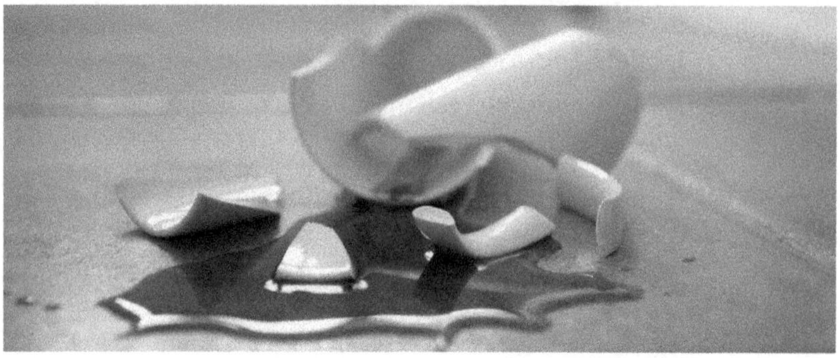

Conversation 1

A I'm so sorry that I broke your coffee mug.

B 1 It's no problem. I didn't really like that mug, anyway.

A 2 ______

B It's OK. These things happen sometimes.

Conversation 2

A I'm so worried.

B 3 ______

A But it looked like Alan really hurt himself.

B 4 ______ The doctors will take good care of him.

A 5 ______

Conversation 3

A I'm so sorry I dropped your scarf and hat in that puddle yesterday.

B 6 ______ I'm just glad you got home before the streets flooded!

A Me, too! And I'll buy you new ones this weekend.

B Thanks, 7 ______

2 REAL-WORLD STRATEGY: Using *at least* to point out the good side of a situation

A **Match the sentences.**

1 I have to work on Friday. b
2 I didn't get the job. ______
3 It's so hot today. ______
4 I didn't get all the classes that I wanted. ______
5 Someone broke my car window. ______

a At least it's not raining like it was yesterday.
b At least you have the weekend off.
c At least you have two other interviews this week.
d At least you were able to get most of them.
e At least they didn't take anything.

3 FUNCTIONAL LANGUAGE AND REAL-WORLD STRATEGY

A **Write a response to each statement with a sentence in the box. The sentences will be used more than once. Then write another response with *at least*. Add your own ideas.**

'll be fine.	Don't worry about it.
These things happen sometimes.	There's no need to worry.

1 **A** Someone crashed into my car yesterday, so I have to walk to work.
B It'll be fine. I walk to work every day, and it's not too bad.
C At least you'll get some exercise.

2 **A** We're late for the 7:00 movie.
B ______
C ______

3 **A** Oh no! I don't have any money, and it's my turn to pay for lunch.
B ______
C ______

4 **A** I forgot to invite Michael to my party. I think I hurt his feelings.
B ______
C ______

5 **A** I lost your sweater! I'm sorry!
B ______
C ______

6 **A** The refrigerator is too full.
B ______
C ______

7 **A** I failed my driving test.
B ______
C ______

4.4 BUSINESS AND PLEASURE

1 LISTENING

A 4.01 LISTEN FOR MAIN IDEAS **Listen to the conversation and check (✓) the <u>five</u> ideas that Sam and David discuss. Underline the idea that they agree on.**

- ☐ a party at Alex's house
- ☐ dinner at David's house
- ☐ a basketball game
- ☐ a day at the beach
- ☐ a party at the community center
- ☐ a concert
- ☐ dinner at a restaurant
- ☐ a party at the park

B 4.01 LISTEN FOR DETAIL **Listen again and write the reasons they say "no" to four of the ideas and "yes" to one idea.**

1 First idea: ______
2 Second idea: ______
3 Third idea: ______
4 Fourth idea: ______
5 Fifth idea: ______

2 READING

A **Read the invitation. Then answer the questions.**

Hey everyone!

Mateo is moving to Costa Rica next month! You're invited to his going away party on June 2nd at the Community Center from noon to 5:00 p.m.!

To start, some of us are going to meet there at 9:00 a.m. to get ready. Please let us know if you can help. We're going to set up the music and a video. At the same time, we're going to make posters and blow up balloons. After that, we're all going to hide so we can be ready to yell "Surprise!" when Mateo arrives. (He thinks he's coming to help Sam clean the floors. ☺)

We're planning to barbecue hamburgers and hot dogs, and we'd like you all to bring something to share. We need salads, desserts, and drinks. There's a pool, so be ready to swim!

We hope you can all come! Remember – this is a surprise, so don't tell Mateo!

David and Sam

Click to reply:

Yes, I'll be there. | No, I won't be there. | Maybe.

1 Where and when is the party? ______
2 Why are they having a party? ______
3 What three things do David and Sam want people to do?
- Bring ______
- Help ______
- Don't ______

3 WRITING

A **Imagine that you are going to have a surprise party for a friend's birthday. Complete the invitation.**

Hey everyone!

You're invited to ____________________'s birthday party! The party is going to be at ____________________ from ____________________.

To start, some of us are going to meet at ____________________ on ____________________ to get ready. Please let us know if you can help.

We're going to ____________________. At the same time, we're going to ____________________. After that, we're all going to ____________________.

We're planning to ____________________, and we'd like you all to bring ____________________.

We hope you can all come! Remember – this is a surprise, so don't tell ____________________!

See you there,

____

CHECK AND REVIEW

Read the statements. Can you do these things?

UNIT 4	Mark the boxes. ☑ I can do it. ? I am not sure. **I can …**	If you are not sure, go back to these pages in the Student's Book.
VOCABULARY	☐ **use adjectives to describe opinions and reactions.**	page 34
	☐ **use verbs and verb phrases for decisions and plans.**	page 36
GRAMMAR	☐ **use *be going to* and *will* for predictions.**	page 35
	☐ **use *will* for sudden decisions and present continuous for future plans.**	page 37
FUNCTIONAL LANGUAGE	☐ **offer reassurance.**	page 38
	☐ **respond to reassurance with *at least*.**	page 39
SKILLS	☐ **write an email describing plans for an event.**	page 41
	☐ **use linking words to show the order of events.**	page 41

UNIT 5 AND THEN ...

5.1 LOST ... AND THEN FOUND

1 VOCABULARY: Losing and finding things

A **Circle the correct words to complete the story.**

Can you imagine losing something and having it [1]*appear / disappear* again a quarter of a century later? April Bolt can. Twenty-five years ago, Bolt [2]*left her purse behind / got her purse back* on a boat on South Carolina's Lake Hartwell. Before she could go back to get it, it [3]*appeared / disappeared*. Maybe it [4]*fell off / dropped* the boat. Or maybe someone picked it up and [5]*fell off / dropped* it in the lake. She [6]*searched for / located* it, but couldn't find it. Just a few months ago, however, 11-year-old Brodie Brooks [7]*discovered / searched for* it while he was fishing on the same lake with his family. When Brooks opened the purse and found the owner's driver's license, his relative Ben Myers recognized the woman in the photo. She was a family friend! Myers [8]*returned / located* Bolt and [9]*left behind / returned* her purse to her. She was shocked that someone found it and was happy to [10]*get it back / leave it behind*.

2 GRAMMAR: Simple past

A **Write the affirmative simple past form of each verb. Then use the past forms of the words to write sentences that are true for you.**

	Present	Past	
1	know	knew	My dad knew I was upset about losing the game.
2	leave		
3	find		
4	take		
5	cry		
6	buy		
7	go		
8	get		

B **Find one error in each question or sentence. Then rewrite it correctly.**

1 How did you lost it? How did you lose it?
2 I find your keys yesterday. ______
3 Did you left it behind somewhere? ______
4 Did he gets his phone back? ______
5 Someone taked my wallet this morning. ______
6 Did you tried to find it? ______
7 I didn't looking for it at school. ______
8 You drop it under your car yesterday? ______

3 GRAMMAR AND VOCABULARY

Question words	Verbs	Nouns
who	discover	backpack
what	drop	~~button~~
where	locate	keys
when	return	phone
how	search for	wallet
why	~~fall off~~	your idea: ________
~~did~~	get back	your idea: ________

A **Write questions in the simple past. Use the ideas in the chart. Add two nouns to the chart.**

1 *Excuse me, did this button fall off your sweater?*
2 ____________________
3 ____________________
4 ____________________
5 ____________________
6 ____________________
7 ____________________

B **Answer the questions from exercise 3A. Include two negative statements.**

1 *Hmm, no, it didn't fall off my sweater. Maybe it fell off the teacher's jacket.*
2 ____________________
3 ____________________
4 ____________________
5 ____________________
6 ____________________
7 ____________________

A button

5.2 HELP FROM A STRANGER

1 VOCABULARY: Needing and giving help

A **Complete each phrase with a word in the box. Write *X* if the phrase does not need another word. Then use the phrases to write sentences that are true for you.**

be	be	break	for	~~give~~	lost	of	out

1 *give* a ride
I gave my friends a ride to the concert.
2 ______ in trouble
______
3 ______ down
______
4 figure ______
______
5 ______ grateful
______
6 get ______
______
7 show ______
______
8 take care ______
______
9 feel sorry ______
______
10 warn ______
______

2 GRAMMAR: Past continuous and simple past

A **For each sentence, underline the events that were in progress and circle the interrupting actions. Then complete two more sentences so they are true for you.**

1 <u>We were getting on the train</u> when (I dropped my phone.)
2 Last night, I heard a noise while I was brushing my teeth.
3 While I was cooking dinner, the phone rang three times.
4 Jack was helping me with my homework when you came over.
5 When I saw you, you were getting on a bus.
6 While I was ______ last week, ______.
7 ______ yesterday when ______.

B **Use the words to make sentences with one event in progress and one interrupting action.**

1 in progress: I / read — interrupting action: James / call
I was reading when James called.

2 in progress: we / study — interrupting action: lights / go out
While ______________________________ ,
______________________________ .

3 interrupting action: I / fall — in progress: I / run for the train
______________________________ while
______________________________ .

4 in progress: I / shop at the mall — interrupting action: I / find a gift for Tom
______________________________ when
______________________________ .

5 in progress: I / read a text — interrupting action: I / miss the bus
While ______________________________ ,
______________________________ .

6 in progress: we / driving — interrupting action: the storm / start
While ______________________________ ,
______________________________ .

3 GRAMMAR AND VOCABULARY

A **Circle the correct phrases to complete the conversations.**

1 **A** I *was sleeping / slept* on the train when someone *woke me up / was waking me up* at the end of the line.
B Wow! I bet you *felt sorry for him / were grateful / were in trouble.*

2 **A** While my nephews *rode / were riding* the roller coaster, it *broke / was breaking.*
B Oh no, it sounds like they *felt sorry for him / were grateful / were in trouble.*

3 **A** I saw your friend *dropped / was dropping* the cake while he *was carrying / carried* it to his girlfriend.
B Yeah, we *felt sorry for him / were grateful / were in trouble.*

B **Complete each sentence. In the first blank, write the correct form of a verb in the box. In the second blank, write your own idea. Remember: use the past continuous, not the simple past, for events that were in progress when something else happened.**

break down | figure out | get lost | give … a ride | ~~take care of~~ | warn

1 My neighbor went on vacation. I was taking care of his cat when it ran outside.
2 Our GPS wasn't working yesterday. We ______________ somewhere in Moscow while we ______________ .
3 I had invitations to two weddings on the same day. When I ______________ what to do, ______________ .
4 I found out there was going to be a big storm. I ______________ all my neighbors about the storm when ______________ .
5 I really need a new car. My car ______________ while I ______________ ,
6 I couldn't find my car keys. My sister ______________ me ______________ to work when ______________ .

5.3 YOU'RE KIDDING!

1 FUNCTIONAL LANGUAGE: Giving and reacting to surprising news

A **Complete the conversation with words and phrases in the box. There are two extra words or phrases.**

can't believe	kidding	never guess	not going to
~~real surprise~~	serious	seriously	true

A So, I had a [1] ___real surprise___ this morning when I was getting ready for class.
B What happened?
A Well, I was watching TV, and you'll [2] ________________ who I saw.
B Who?
A It was Eduardo from our math class last year.
B You're [3] ________________! Why was he on TV?
A He plays guitar in a band! And they're famous!
B Famous? Are you [4] ________________? I didn't even know he was a musician.
A I didn't know either. And you're [5] ________________ believe this. He writes all the songs!
B Wow, that's amazing!
A I know. I [6] ________________ it.

2 REAL-WORLD STRATEGY: Repeating words to express surprise

A **Circle the repeated words that best express surprise.**

1 **A** I'm visiting my sister in Tokyo for the weekend!
B *(In Tokyo?) / Visiting your sister?*

2 **A** I earned $500 in tips at work today!
B *At work? / $500?*

3 **A** Rosa was skiing and she broke her leg!
B *Broke her leg? / Skiing?*

4 **A** I saw an old friend today for the first time in ten years!
B *An old friend? / Ten years?*

5 **A** Wow, I walked 12 miles yesterday.
B *Twelve miles? / Yesterday?*

3 FUNCTIONAL LANGUAGE AND REAL-WORLD STRATEGY

A **Respond to each piece of surprising news. Use an expression for reacting with surprise and repeated words.**

1 **A** You'll never guess who I saw when I was shopping today! I saw Angelina Jolie!
B *Angelina Jolie? Are you serious?*
A Yes! It was so exciting. But I lost my phone, so I couldn't take a picture.

2 **A** You're not going to believe this. I found a diamond ring in the park when I was running this morning.
B ______
A Yeah, but I think I'm going to take it to the police station.

3 **A** I had a real surprise this morning. Remember the ring I lost last year? I found it in a jar of pickles!
B ______
A Yes, it was so funny.

4 **A** I can't believe it. I had such a hard time this semester, but I got As in all of my classes.
B ______
A Uh-huh, I feel so good about it!

5 **A** You're not going to believe this. Someone took my wallet when I was at the police station.
B ______
A Yeah, I was shocked. The police were really helpful, though.

B **Write short conversations about surprising things that happened to you. Include expressions for giving surprising news, expressions for reacting with surprise, and repeated words. You can use the ideas given or your own ideas.**

saw someone you knew a long time ago | found something valuable | won a game or contest

Conversation 1
A ______
B ______

Conversation 2
A ______
B ______

Conversation 3
A ______
B ______

5.4 STORYTELLING

1 READING

A **READ FOR DETAIL** **Read Anna's story. Then read the statements and check (✓) *True*, *False*, or *Not given*.**

When I was young, I was afraid of the dark, so I always slept with a small table lamp on. One night, I couldn't sleep. I got out of bed and went to the kitchen to get a glass of water. When I came back into my room, I stepped on something. As I fell onto the floor, the glass of water flew out of my hand, and the light went out. It was so dark and I was so scared. I was sure that there was a monster in my room and that I stepped on its foot! I screamed and screamed. My parents came running into the room to see what was wrong. By then I was crying and I couldn't really talk. My father turned my bedroom light on, and my mother picked me up off the floor and put me into my bed. After I calmed down, I said that a monster turned my lamp off when I stepped on its foot. Then my father bent over and picked something up. It was a stuffed animal! I tripped on it and accidentally unplugged the lamp as I fell down! We all laughed and laughed about it. Then my parents plugged my lamp back in and cleaned all the water off my floor.

	True	False	Not given
1 The writer was afraid of the dark.	☐	☐	☐
2 She couldn't sleep because she was afraid.	☐	☐	☐
3 When the light went out, she got back into bed.	☐	☐	☐
4 Her parents came in when they heard her screaming.	☐	☐	☐
5 She fell because she stepped on some water.	☐	☐	☐

2 LISTENING

A 5.01 **Listen to two people discussing the story in exercise 1A. Then answer the questions.**

1 What does Karen think of Anna's story?

____

2 Which of the four *Ss* does Karen think Anna did not include?

____

3 How does Karen think Anna should change her story?

____

4 What did Karen think Anna stepped on in the story?

____

3 WRITING

A **Write a short story like the one in exercise 1A. It can be true or you can make it up. Remember the four Ss: *simple*; *shared experiences*; *show, don't tell*; and *surprise*.**

When I was young, I was afraid of ____________________, so I always ____________________

____

____

____

____

____

____

____

____

____

____

____

____

____

____

____

CHECK AND REVIEW

Read the statements. Can you do these things?

UNIT 5	Mark the boxes. ☑ I can do it. ? I am not sure.		If you are not sure, go back to these pages in the Student's Book.
		I can …	
VOCABULARY	☐	**use verbs for losing and finding things.**	page 44
	☐	**use verbs for needing and giving help.**	page 46
GRAMMAR	☐	**use the simple past.**	page 45
	☐	**use the past continuous and the simple past.**	page 47
FUNCTIONAL LANGUAGE	☐	**give and react to surprising news.**	page 48
	☐	**repeat words to express surprise.**	page 49
SKILLS	☐	**write a short story.**	page 51
	☐	**use storytelling expressions.**	page 51

6.1 MOVING TO A MEGACITY

1 VOCABULARY: Urban problems

A **Use the clues to complete the crossword puzzle.**

ACROSS

3 Factories can cause ______ in the water.

5 Old candy wrappers and used tissues are ______ .

7 We all want to breathe clean ______ .

8 If something burns, it makes ______ .

9 A picture spray-painted on the wall of a building is called ______ .

DOWN

1 There is not a lot of open ______ in big cities. It's all covered by buildings and roads.

2 Sidewalks are made of ______ .

4 In a ______ , cars move very slowly or not at all.

5 There is a lot of ______ on the roads when everyone is on their way to work.

6 Big cities are not usually quiet – there is a lot of ______ .

8 City apartments are usually small because there isn't a lot of ______ for big apartments.

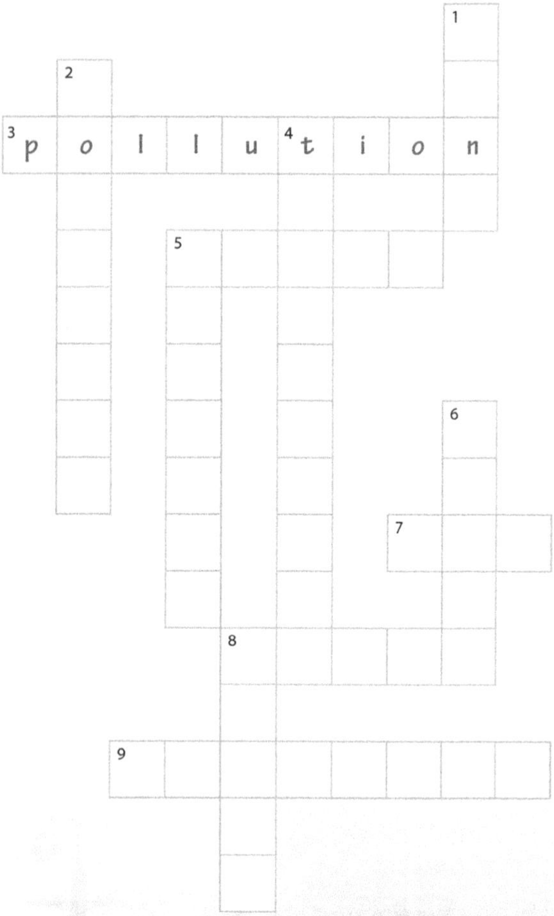

2 GRAMMAR: Quantifiers

A **Put each word in the box in the correct place in the chart.**

~~air~~	car	graffiti	noise	road	space	train
~~building~~	concrete	highway	office	sidewalk	traffic	trash
bus	color	land	pollution	smoke	traffic jam	tree

Count nouns	Noncount nouns
building	*air*

B **Correct the sentences.**

1 There are so ~~much~~ *many* people in this city.

2 Almost all of the peoples here live in apartments.

3 There is very few space left for new people.

4 There is almost no trashes on the streets in my neighborhood.

5 Several of the building downtown have graffiti on them.

6 There is so many graffiti on the building where I work.

7 Almost no of the real color of the building shows.

3 GRAMMAR AND VOCABULARY

A **Write sentences with quantifiers about the place where you live. Use three count nouns and three noncount nouns from exercise 2A.**

1 *There are so few tall buildings in my hometown.*

2 ___

3 ___

4 ___

5 ___

6 ___

7 ___

6.2 INTELLIGENT SOLUTIONS

1 VOCABULARY: Adverbs of manner

A **Choose all of the adverbs that you can use with each verb or verb phrase.**

1 speak

☐ angrily ☐ completely ☐ politely
☐ clearly ☐ loudly ☐ safely

2 drive

☐ angrily ☐ correctly ☐ loudly
☐ clearly ☐ dangerously ☐ safely

3 play the piano

☐ beautifully ☐ correctly ☐ loudly
☐ completely ☐ dangerously ☐ safely

4 explain something

☐ calmly ☐ completely ☐ politely
☐ clearly ☐ correctly ☐ safely

5 answer a question

☐ calmly ☐ completely ☐ dangerously
☐ clearly ☐ correctly ☐ politely

2 GRAMMAR: Present and future real conditionals

A **Circle the correct words to complete the sentences.**

1 If there *won't be / aren't* any trash cans in the city, people *will throw / throw* their garbage on the street.
2 When there *is / will be* a lot of trash on the street, a city *looks / will look* ugly.
3 The city *looks / will look* great in the summer *if / when* we clean it up now.
4 When it *is / will be* hot outside, the trash *starts / starting* to smell bad.
5 People *move / will move* away if we *will take / don't take* care of our city.
6 If the city *will get / gets* more polluted than it is now, visitors *don't want / won't want* to come here.
7 If we *are keeping / keep* our parks clean, more people *will go / go* to them.
8 When lots of people *use / will use* a public space, the city usually *is spending / spends* more money to maintain it.
9 Musicians *will come / are coming* to perform concerts in a park if it *will be / is* clean, popular, and beautiful.

3 GRAMMAR AND VOCABULARY

A **Match the sentence halves. Then write *P* after the present real sentences and *F* after the future real sentences.**

1 If you don't write clearly, ___b___
2 If you speak angrily, ______
3 If you drive safely, ______
4 If you drive dangerously, ______
5 If you answer the test questions completely, ______
6 If you speak politely, ______
7 If people play their music loudly, ______

a you will probably get an A on the test. ______
b the teacher won't be able to read your writing. ___F___
c people will want to listen to you. ______
d no one wants to hear what you have to say. ______
e you might injure yourself or someone else. ______
f their neighbors get upset. ______
g you don't have accidents. ______

B **Change the *if* clauses from exercise 3A to express the opposite idea. Then write new results.**

1 *If you write clearly, your classmates will be able to follow your notes.*
2 ______
3 ______
4 ______
5 ______
6 ______
7 ______

C **Complete the sentences. Use present real or future real conditionals and adverbs of manner.**

1 Children ______ if they ask ______.
2 In my city, people ______ when they ride bikes ______.
3 Other passengers ______ if someone is not speaking ______ on the bus.
4 When people explain problems ______, it is easier to ______.
5 If I speak ______, my co-workers ______ my presentation.

6.3 BREAKDOWN

1 FUNCTIONAL LANGUAGE: Expressing concern and relief

A **Complete the conversations with the sentences in the boxes.**

Conversation 1

Are you all right? What a relief! Is anything wrong?

A [1] ______________________

B I had a terrible night last night. My apartment building caught on fire.

A Oh no! [2] ______________________

B Yeah, the fire was pretty bad, but I'm OK. My neighbors are all right, too.

A [3] ______________________

Conversation 2

That's such a relief! I'm glad to hear that. I was really worried. Is everyone OK?

A Hey, I heard there was an earthquake near you last night. [4] ______________________

B Thanks for calling. Yeah, we're all OK.

A [5] ______________________ Did your house get damaged?

B No, it's fine. A few things fell off of shelves, but that's all.

A [6] ______________________ [7] ______________________

2 REAL-WORLD STRATEGY: Using *though* to give a contrasting idea

A **Add *though* to the sentences where it is appropriate. Remember to include a comma.**

1 No one got hurt. It was scary, though.

2 I fell on the beach and hurt my arm. I didn't break it. The sand was soft.

3 My car broke down on the highway. It doesn't have any major problems. It just ran out of gas.

4 The fire was really bad. The whole building burned down. No one was hurt.

5 There was a huge accident on the highway. We were stuck in traffic for two hours. We had a good conversation in the car.

6 I missed my bus this morning. I got to work on time. My friend saw me at the bus stop and gave me a ride.

B **Imagine that you are describing the situations to someone. Write sentences with *though*.**

1 Your bus crashed. You all had to stay on the bus for an hour. No one was hurt.

My bus crashed, and we all had to stay on the bus for an hour. No one was hurt, though.

2 You fell on an icy sidewalk. You scratched your leg. You didn't break it.

______

3 You cut your hand. It looked bad. You didn't have to go to the hospital.

______

4 A lot of people got sick from eating bad shrimp at your office party. You didn't get sick. You didn't have any shrimp.

______

5 You got lost on your vacation. You had a great time. You met some nice people.

______

3 FUNCTIONAL LANGUAGE AND REAL-WORLD STRATEGY

A **Put the conversations in order.**

Conversation 1

B I'm fine. My bike is broken, though. ____

A That's a relief. ____

B Yeah, I just need to buy some new parts. ____

A Are you all right? I heard you had a bicycle accident. ____

A Oh no! Can you fix it? ____

Conversation 2

B Why? What happened? ____

A I saw an ambulance in front of your house today. Is anything wrong? ____

B No, we're fine. ____

A None of us was hurt. The ambulance driver is in trouble, though. ____

B He drove to the wrong house! ____

A What a relief! I was really worried. ____

B **Complete the conversation with *though* and expressions of concern and relief.**

A 1 ______ Lee saw you at the hospital today. 2 ______

B Thanks, I'm fine. I was just visiting my sister.

A 3 ______ But I hope your sister is OK.

B She was really sick. She's feeling a lot better now, 4 ______ .

A 5 ______

6.4 BEATING THE TRAFFIC

1 LISTENING

A 6.01 LISTEN FOR DETAIL **Listen to the podcast. Choose the correct answers.**

1 What is the podcast about?
  a self-driving cars **b** underwater cars **c** flying cars
2 What is Teresa designing a car for?
  a emergencies **b** entertainment **c** to solve traffic problems
3 Does she think everyone will have one of these cars?
  a Yes. **b** No. **c** She's not sure.
4 When does Teresa think we will have these cars?
  a in a few years **b** in several years **c** never

B 6.01 **Read each line from the podcast. Who said it? Check (✓) *Steve* or *Teresa*. Then listen to the podcast again to check your answers.**

		Steve	Teresa
1	A lot of sci-fi movies show people driving around in the sky.	☐	☐
2	My goal is to develop flying cars for emergencies.	☐	☐
3	… do you think flying cars will solve our traffic problems?	☐	☐
4	Can you tell us why?	☐	☐
5	Flying ambulances won't have that problem.	☐	☐
6	We still have a lot of work to do …	☐	☐

2 READING

A **Read the comment by a podcast listener, Opinionzzz. Check (✓) the problems that he writes about. Circle the ones that Steve and Teresa already mentioned.**

Opinionzzz wrote:

I hope we never have flying cars of any kind. I think even flying ambulances are a bad idea. Why? Well, first of all, if everyone is flying cars in the sky, we'll have traffic jams in the air! And imagine a car accident in the air – flying car parts might fall onto people on the ground. People in the flying cars might even fall out!

Second, we already have a lot of air pollution. I think that flying cars would create more of it. The air in big cities would be horrible.

Third, cars break down all the time. When your car breaks down, you just pull over to the side of the road. What will you do if your car breaks down in the air? Your car would probably just fall to the ground. That might destroy your car and even hurt someone else … or worse.

I definitely don't think we should have flying cars. Let's find other ways to get ambulances to people more quickly.

☐ flying too fast
☐ traffic in the sky
☐ expensive cost of cars
☐ cars breaking down
☐ falling out of the sky
☐ too much noise
☐ air pollution
☐ being afraid of flying

3 WRITING

A **Write your own comment responding to Steve's podcast and Opinionzzz's comment. Decide if you think flying ambulances are a good idea or not. Give reasons and use questions to make points.**

CHECK AND REVIEW

Read the statements. Can you do these things?

UNIT 6	Mark the boxes. ☑ I can do it. ? I am not sure. **I can …**	If you are not sure, go back to these pages in the Student's Book.
VOCABULARY	☐ **use nouns to talk about urban problems.** ☐ **use adverbs of manner.**	page 54 page 56
GRAMMAR	☐ **use quantifiers.** ☐ **use present and future real conditionals.**	page 55 page 57
FUNCTIONAL LANGUAGE	☐ **express concern and relief.** ☐ **use *though* to give a contrasting idea.**	page 58 page 59
SKILLS	☐ **write a post giving your point of view.** ☐ **use questions to make points.**	page 61 page 61

7.1 A 50-YEAR PLAYLIST

1 VOCABULARY: Music

A **Find 9 more vocabulary words in the word search.**

classical country ~~EDM~~ folk heavymetal hip-hop jazz pop reggae rock

C	D	L	A	B	H	R	T	I	M	W	X	P	D	E	R	Y
A	C	O	U	N	T	R	Y	N	S	N	H	E	K	M	F	O
C	E	Y	V	D	F	E	U	S	Q	K	F	W	C	P	O	P
E	X	E	E	K	W	C	D	E	L	V	R	U	O	S	L	E
B	H	E	C	R	O	S	Q	A	H	E	V	Y	B	E	K	P
S	I	L	J	R	E	G	G	A	E	S	Y	V	B	U	W	X
H	P	C	U	R	F	K	L	W	A	B	E	D	M	R	P	E
D	H	L	W	J	X	U	S	F	V	K	E	H	D	W	C	J
Q	O	U	J	A	Z	Z	E	C	Y	H	O	L	L	W	E	B
M	P	S	A	L	O	M	S	W	M	A	J	I	E	C	R	L
K	E	D	V	Y	E	W	H	I	E	C	Y	G	N	R	E	I
T	R	T	S	I	V	A	R	E	T	E	C	H	N	O	D	A
S	T	A	S	K	W	L	O	E	A	S	B	E	Y	C	M	Q
W	C	L	A	S	S	I	C	A	L	S	X	Y	N	K	B	I
X	T	R	O	N	W	C	I	S	U	D	D	U	M	T	H	Y

2 GRAMMAR: *used to*

A **Complete each sentence with the subject and verb in parentheses ( ). Add the correct form of *used to*.**

1 A Where *did you use to buy* your music? (you / buy)

B ______________ it in music stores. (I / get)

2 A ______________ to rock music when he was a teenager? (he / listen)

B No, ______________ rock music. (he / not like)

3 A What kind of music ______________ when she was young? (your mother / like)

B ______________ heavy metal. (she / love) ______________ classical music, but she likes it now. (she / not listen to)

4 A ______________ to a lot of concerts before you were born? (your parents / go)

B No, concerts were expensive. But ______________ a lot of jazz CDs and listen to them together. (they / buy)

5 A "I Want You Back" by *NSYNC ______________ my favorite song when I was in high school. (be)

B ______________ that pop song! (I / hate) ______________ it on the radio constantly! (they / play)

B **Circle the correct words to complete the sentences.**

1 I *used to go* / *went* to a dance class three times a week, but I hated the music we had to dance to!
2 I *used to come* / *came* home at 6:00 a.m. after the New Year's Eve dance party in 2016.
3 My aunt and uncle *didn't use to sing* / *didn't sing* "Happy Birthday" to my cousin when she turned three. They completely forgot!
4 My best friend *used to make* / *made* the best playlists before we studied for all of our big tests.

3 GRAMMAR AND VOCABULARY

A **Complete each sentence with the correct form of *used to*, the verb in parentheses ( ), and a word or phrase in the box.**

~~classical~~ EDM heavy metal jazz pop hip-hop reggae

1 Susan used to listen to classical music a lot because she played piano and violin. (listen to)
2 Jack ____________, but now he thinks it's too loud and the singers sound like they're screaming. (enjoy)
3 Eric ____________ music because it was so fast and he couldn't understand the words. (not like)
4 Sam ____________, but after his vacation to Jamaica, he started to listen to it all the time. His favorite singer is Bob Marley. (not listen to)
5 Linda's grandfather ____________ in the 1930s. He was the saxophone player in a band. (play)
6 I ____________ music, but I don't like it anymore. I deleted all the Katy Perry and Britney Spears songs from my music app. (like)
7 My friends ____________, but then I took them to some dance clubs, and now they love it! (not care about)

B **Correct the mistake in each sentence.**

1 My friends and I use to go to concerts a lot. My friends and I used to go to concerts a lot.
2 Did you used to listen to pop music? ____________
3 I wasn't use to like reggae. ____________
4 Where did you usually use to listen to music? ____________
5 Do you use to have a favorite band? ____________
6 What kind of music do your favorite band used to play? ____________

C **Answer the questions in exercise 3B and add details. For the statements, rewrite them as questions.**

1 Did you and your friends use to go to concerts a lot?
2 ____________
3 ____________
4 ____________
5 ____________
6 ____________

7.2 THE BEST ENTERTAINMENT

1 VOCABULARY: TV shows and movies

A **Match the words with the correct TV or movie genre.**

1 information, real, learn ____ a comedy
2 prize, games, host ____ b documentary
3 frightening, suspense, surprise ending ____ c game show
4 entertain, laugh, jokes ____ d science fiction
5 imaginary, future, technology ____ e thriller

B **Complete the sentences with the correct words or phrases in the box.**

comedy	horror	game show	~~documentary~~
musicals	reality show	talk show	

1 We watched a *documentary* about climate change in my biology class.
2 My friend won $5,000 on a ____. She answered all the questions correctly.
3 Do you watch this ____? It always has good guests, and the host is so funny.
4 I can't watch ____ movies when I'm home alone. I get too scared.
5 I like to watch ____ shows when I come home from work. They make me laugh.
6 I don't ever want to be on a ____. My life is private.
7 I like ____ if the songs are good.

C **Complete the sentences with the correct words or phrases in the box.**

animated movies	soap opera	dramas	romantic comedies	science fiction	thrillers

1 *Star Wars* is the first ____ movie that I saw.
2 That actor is in a lot of ____. He usually plays a police officer or a spy.
3 I like to make digital drawings. I want to make ____ when I'm finished with school.
4 Sometimes I don't like to watch ____ because they're too serious for me.
5 Gina likes to watch her favorite ____ every day at 2:00. The characters are always fighting or falling in love.
6 Some people think only women like ____, but I know a lot of men who like funny movies about people falling in love.

2 GRAMMAR: Comparisons with *(not) as … as*

A **Unscramble the words to make sentences with *not as … as*.**

1 as / not / The second / good / first movie / as / the / movie is / .

2 like the / you / season / season / as / second / much / the first / Did / as / ?

3 movie is / good / The / as / not / the book / as / .

4 shows have / dramas / as / as / Reality / excitement / much / .

3 GRAMMAR AND VOCABULARY

A **Read the situations. Then write sentences with the words in parentheses ( ) and *(not) as … as*.**

1 She always likes learning things. She sometimes likes scary movies.
(not like / horror movies / documentaries)
She doesn't like horror movies as much as documentaries.

2 It's kind of fun to watch people talk. It's a lot of fun to watch people answer questions for money.
(talk shows / not fun / game shows)

3 I like watching serious movies. I also like watching movies about space or the future.
(like / dramas / science fiction movies)

4 Movies about crime and spies are really exciting. Scary movies are also really exciting.
(thrillers / exciting / horror movies)

B **Write sentences with *(not) as … as* that are true for you. Use the words in parentheses ( ) from exercise 3A. Add details.**

1 *I don't like documentaries as much as horror movies. Horror movies are much more exciting!*

2

3

4

7.3 A NEW BAND

1 FUNCTIONAL LANGUAGE: Refusing invitations and responding to refusals

A **Put the conversations in order.**

Conversation 1

B I'm sorry. Unfortunately, I have plans on Sunday. ____
B I'd love to, but I have to work on Saturday. ____
A I understand. Let me know if your plans change. ____
A Do you want to go out to dinner on Saturday night? ____
A Oh, that's too bad. How about lunch on Sunday? ____

Conversation 2

B I think I want to stay home on Friday. But thanks for asking. ____
B I have to finish my paper right now. Maybe after that. ____
A Yeah. I need to buy some new shoes. ____
A I understand. Let me know if you change your mind. ____
B Right now? ____
A Do you want to go shopping with me? ____
A OK. Oh, are you free on Friday? Jack and I are going to the movies. ____

2 REAL-WORLD STRATEGY: Softening comments

A **Soften each comment with *kind of* or *sort of.***

1 Unfortunately, I'm busy tonight.

____

2 I'd love to, but I'm tired.

____

3 I'm sorry, but I think romantic comedies are silly.

____

4 No thanks. I think talk shows are boring.

____

5 Unfortunately, it's late.

____

3 FUNCTIONAL LANGUAGE AND REAL-WORLD STRATEGY

A **Write conversations using the ideas in the pictures. One speaker makes an invitation and the other speaker refuses the invitation. Soften the refusals.**

Conversation 1

A *Do you want to see a romantic comedy with me tonight?*

B

A

Conversation 2

A

B

A

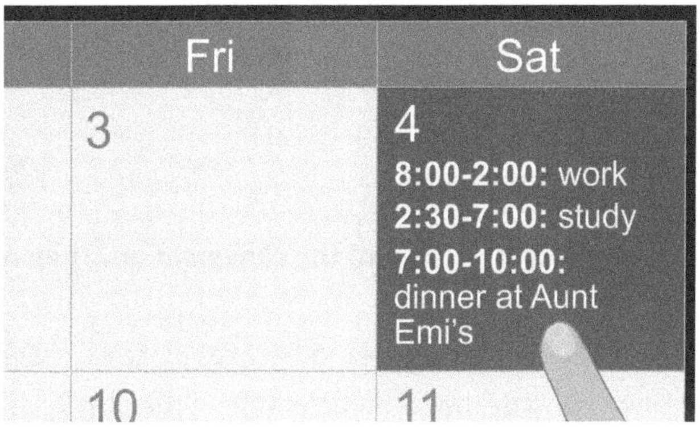

Conversation 3

A

B

A

7.4 NOT JUST FOR KIDS

1 READING

A READ FOR DETAIL **Read the article and complete the sentences with information from the text.**

Why Do We Binge-Watch TV Shows?

How do you watch shows? Do you watch one episode a week? One a day? Or do you sometimes watch entire seasons in a weekend? If you like watching episode after episode of a series, you're not alone. Binge-watching has become more and more popular in the past few years. But why?

STRESS RELIEF When we binge-watch, we escape from our real lives for a few hours. While we're watching, we don't think about our problems or responsibilities. That can help us relieve stress.

HAPPINESS According to experts, when we binge-watch, our brains produce *dopamine* – a chemical that makes us feel happy. As soon as one episode is over, we start the next one because we want to keep feeling good.

CARING Psychologists say that our brains can experience things we watch on TV almost the same way that they experience real events. So we often become attached to stories and characters and really care about what happens to them. Because our brains aren't always good at separating episodes on TV from real life events, we have a strong desire to keep watching to find out what happens next.

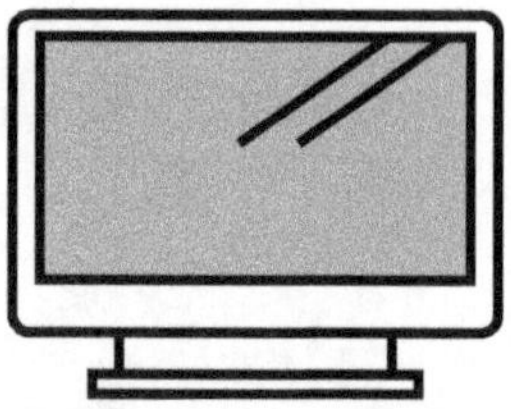

Based on this information, it seems like binge-watching is a good thing – at least in the short term. However, over time, experts say that it can cause depression. When we finish binge-watching a series, we can feel a sense of loss. We can also feel sad because our brains stop producing dopamine.

1 When we binge-watch, we can forget about our ______ and ______.
2 Binge-watching helps us get rid of ______.
3 Binge-watching makes us feel ______.
4 When we see something happen in a TV show, our brains think we're experiencing it ______.
5 We can get really attached to the ______ and ______ in a show.

B **Do you think it's a good idea to binge-watch shows? Why or why not?**

______

______

2 LISTENING

A 7.01 **Listen to the conversation. Then read the statements and check (✓) *True*, *False*, or *Not given*.**

	True	False	Not given
1 Ken's favorite movie takes place on a weekday.	☐	☐	☐
2 The main characters are in the same class.	☐	☐	☐
3 The story takes place in the school cafeteria.	☐	☐	☐
4 It's a musical.	☐	☐	☐
5 The movie shows us that people are alike.	☐	☐	☐

3 WRITING

A **Write a conversation in which you recommend a movie you have seen to a friend. Include the kind of movie it is, a short description, and at least three reasons why you like it.**

A ______________________________

____

B ______________________________

____

A ______________________________

____

B ______________________________

____

A ______________________________

____

B ______________________________

____

A ______________________________

____

B ______________________________

____

A ______________________________

____

B ______________________________

____

CHECK AND REVIEW

Read the statements. Can you do these things?

UNIT 7	Mark the boxes.	☑ I can do it. ? I am not sure. **I can …**	If you are not sure, go back to these pages in the Student's Book.
	VOCABULARY	☐ **talk about different types of music.** ☐ **talk about TV shows and movies.**	page 66 page 68
	GRAMMAR	☐ **use *used to*.** ☐ **make comparisons with *(not) as … as*.**	page 67 page 69
	FUNCTIONAL LANGUAGE	☐ **refuse invitations.** ☐ **respond to refusals.** ☐ **soften comments.**	page 70 page 70 page 71
	SKILLS	☐ **write a movie review.** ☐ **organize ideas.**	page 73 page 73

UNIT 8 GETTING THERE

8.1 SAYING AND DOING

1 VOCABULARY: Describing experiences

A **Match each word with its definition.**

1 achievement ___d___
2 challenge ______
3 change ______
4 opportunity ______
5 project ______

a a chance to do something
b a difficult task
c a planned task
d a particular thing that you have done successfully
e something different from what you were doing before

B **Match more words with their definitions.**

1 chore ______
2 process ______
3 job ______
4 success ______

a an attempt that ends in a good result
b something that you do to make money
c an ordinary task that you do regularly, like cleaning
d the steps involved in doing something

2 GRAMMAR: Present perfect continuous

A **Complete each question with a word or phrase in the box. Then answer the questions so they are true for you.**

Has	Have	I	someone in your class
What has	~~Where have~~	your mom and dad	

1 A ___Where have___ you been working?
B I've been working in the library, but on Saturdays I work in a café.

2 A ______________ 've been working a lot. What about you?
B ______________

3 A Have ______________ been reading a lot of books lately?
B ______________

4 A ______________ your best friend been doing this week?
B ______________

5 A Has ______________ been learning how to cook?
B ______________

6 A ______________ you been taking music lessons recently?
B ______________

7 A ______________ anyone been calling or texting you every day?
B ______________

B **Complete the sentences with the subjects and the present perfect continuous forms of the verbs in parentheses ( ).**

1 What _have you been doing_ these past few days? (you / do)
2 ______ a Spanish class. (I / take)
3 ______ how to paint. (she / learn)
4 ______ out a lot? (you and your friends / go)
5 ______ a lot this summer. (we / travel)
6 ______ all afternoon. (he / call)

3 GRAMMAR AND VOCABULARY

A **Complete the sentences with the present perfect continuous form of the verbs in parentheses ( ) and a word in the box.**

achievement ~~chores~~ job process project

1 He _has been doing_ _chores_ at home all morning – vacuuming, doing laundry, washing dishes. (do)
2 I ______ on a new ______ at the office. It's almost finished. (work)
3 I ______ about the ______ of creating a handmade book. There are a lot of steps. (learn)
4 I ______ for a new ______. I'm not happy at work. (look)
5 She ______ hard for this ______. She just graduated from college. (work)

B **Answer the questions. Give examples.**

1 What opportunities have you been taking advantage of lately?

2 What have you been having the most success at lately: school, home, or work? Explain.

3 What kinds of challenges have you been dealing with in your academic or professional life lately?

8.2 STARTED, BUT NOT FINISHED

1 VOCABULARY: Describing progress

A **Write each phrase in the correct place in the chart.**

concentrating on	didn't have a chance	doing my best	getting nowhere
~~having problems~~	having trouble	making good progress	taking it easy

Fast or focused progress	Slow or no progress
	having problems

B **Complete the conversation with the correct forms of the verbs in the box.**

have save spend waste

A You've been [1] ________________ a lot of time working on your new website lately, haven't you?
B Yeah, I learned how to code, so I can [2] ________________ time and work more quickly.
A That's great. Do you think you'll [3] ________________ time to help me with my website?
B Well, not today. My computer crashed! I've [4] ________________ a lot of time trying to fix it. I can't figure it out.

2 GRAMMAR: Present perfect vs. present perfect continuous

A **Circle the correct verb form to complete each sentence.**

1. I've *looked* / *been looking* for a new job for the past month.
2. I've *had* / *been having* three job interviews so far.
3. I've *worked* / *been working* part-time during my job search.
4. She's *gone* / *been going* to the supermarket five times this week.
5. She's *tried* / *been trying* new recipes since she started her cooking classes.
6. She's *taken* / *been taking* cooking classes for a few months.

B **Find and correct mistakes in <u>four</u> of the sentences. If a sentence is correct, write *correct*.**

1 I've read three books this month.

correct

2 She been spending a lot of time with her family lately.

3 We've clean the whole house.

4 I've been worked all day.

5 He have gone to Hong Kong twice.

6 We've been traveling for a week.

3 GRAMMAR AND VOCABULARY

A **Complete each sentence with the present perfect or present perfect continuous form of the verb in parentheses ( ) and a word or phrase in the box.**

a chance	a lot of time	it easy	my best	nowhere

1 I decided that I need a break, so I ______________ lately. (take)

2 I ______________, but I still can't work as quickly as you can. I'll keep trying. (do)

3 Oh no! This is the wrong paint! I ______________. Now I have to paint all the walls again. (waste)

4 I ______________ on this project after three days of work, so I'm moving onto a different one. (get)

5 I ______________ to read this book yet, but I'm going to start reading it tonight. (not / have)

B **Answer the questions.**

1 When you're having trouble at work or school, who do you talk to about it? Why?

2 Do you know a way to save a lot of time at work, at home, or on the way to work? Describe one way.

3 Where do you go when you have to concentrate on work or schoolwork and you don't want anyone to bother you?

8.3 HOW HAVE YOU BEEN?

1 FUNCTIONAL LANGUAGE: Talking to someone you haven't seen in a while

A **Put the conversations in order.**

Conversation 1

B I know. I haven't seen you since last summer! ____

B Good, thanks. What have you been up to? ____

A Hi, Mateo! It's been a long time. ____

B The same as usual. ____

A So, how have you been? ____

A Not much. I've just been going to school. What's going on with you? ____

Conversation 2

A The same as usual. She works all the time. What have you been up to? ____

A I've been really busy. I have to travel a lot for my job. Oh, hey, I saw Dasha last month. ____

B Not much. I've been looking for a new job. ____

A It's great to see you again, Melinda! It's been a long time. ____

B I know. What have you been doing? ____

B Really? What's going on with her? ____

2 REAL-WORLD STRATEGY: Using *that would be* to comment on something

A **Write a comment about each statement using *that would be* and the best adjective in the box.**

awful   exciting   fun   great   interesting

1 **A** I heard that Alan might lose his job.
  B ____________________. He really needs that job.

2 **A** Do you want to have lunch at Luigi's Italian restaurant tomorrow?
  B ____________________. I love Luigi's.

3 **A** Sook and I are going ice-skating tomorrow. Do you want to join us?
  B ____________________. Sook always makes me laugh.

4 **A** I'm thinking about going on a trip around the world.
  B ____________________. You should do it!

5 **A** Do you want to come with me to a lecture about space travel?
  B ____________________. I read a lot of books about the future of space travel.

3 FUNCTIONAL LANGUAGE AND REAL-WORLD STRATEGY

A **Read the situations. Complete the sentences with phrases from the box.**

have you been	haven't seen you	it's been
the same as	too much	what have you

- You see someone you knew when you were 10 years old.
  Hey, [1] ________________ a long time! How [2] ________________ ?
- You run into an old classmate.
  Wow, I [3] ________________ since last semester! [4] ________________ been up to?
- An old teacher asks you what you've been doing since last year.
  Oh, not [5] ________________ . Just [6] ________________ usual.

B **Complete the conversation with expressions for catching up with people's news or comments with *that would be*.**

A Hi, it's so great to see you. [1] ________________ .

B I know! [2] ________________ since last spring when we had that class together.

A I can't believe we ran into each other here. [3] ________________ ?

B [4] ________________ . I'm still going to school, and I've been working full-time since July. [5] ________________ ?

A Oh, [6] ________________ . I've been taking classes full-time. Hey, are you busy right now? Do you want to get some dinner?

B [7] ________________ . Where should we go?

A Well, I've been thinking about Chinese food all day because someone in my office was eating some.

B Oh, I know a fantastic Chinese restaurant. You don't order your food. The servers just bring you whatever the chef is cooking.

A [8] ________________ .

B Great! Let's go!

8.4 A TIME-SAVING TIP

1 LISTENING

A 8.01 LISTEN FOR MAIN AND SUPPORTING IDEAS **Listen to the podcast. Answer the questions.**

1 What is the first tip? ______

2 What is an example of the first tip? ______

3 How is the first tip helpful for Tina? ______

4 What is the second tip? ______

5 How is the second tip helpful for Tina? ______

6 According to Andrew, which of the two tips can save you more time? ______

2 READING

A **Read the comment by BusyBee221. Then read the statements and check (✓) the ones that are true.**

BusyBee221 wrote:

After I listened to the latest episode of *Tips with Tina*, I immediately decided to try Andrew's tips for saving time. Like Tina, I'm always losing my keys. I also spend a lot of time looking for my wallet in the morning. So, I put a bowl on the dresser in my bedroom, and I started putting my keys and my wallet in it when I got home every evening. I tried it for a week, and it really made a difference. Before, I used to feel rushed every morning, and I would sometimes get to class late, but now I don't feel rushed at all. I got to class on time every day last week, and I even had time to stop for coffee on my way to school.

The second tip was harder to follow, but I did my best. I managed to say "no" to one invitation last week when my friend invited me to a movie. I felt guilty about it for a while, but I was really glad that I refused the invitation. While my friend was at the movies, I finished my paper for my history class. It felt great!

So far, Andrew's tips are working for me. I think they'll keep saving me time in the future.

reply

☐ 1 BusyBee221 tried Andrew's tips.

☐ 2 He started putting his wallet and keys in a bowl by the front door.

☐ 3 He didn't have to look for his keys, but he still got to class late every morning.

☐ 4 He said "no" to one friend's invitation.

☐ 5 He was able to write a paper because he didn't go to the movies with his friend.

☐ 6 He wishes that he had said "yes" to his friend.

3 WRITING

A **Write your own comment responding to Tina's podcast and BusyBee221's comment. Decide if you think Andrew's tips are helpful.**

CHECK AND REVIEW

Read the statements. Can you do these things?

UNIT 8	Mark the boxes. ☑ I can do it. ? I am not sure. **I can …**	If you are not sure, go back to these pages in the Student's Book.
VOCABULARY	☐ **describe experiences.** ☐ **describe progress.**	page 76 page 78
GRAMMAR	☐ **use the present perfect continuous.** ☐ **use the present perfect and the present perfect continuous.**	page 77 page 79
FUNCTIONAL LANGUAGE	☐ **ask about someone's news and say how long it's been.** ☐ **use *that would be* to comment on something.**	page 80 page 81
SKILLS	☐ **write a post about managing your time.** ☐ **use time expressions.**	page 83 page 83

UNIT 9 MAKE IT WORK

9.1 BUILDING A FUTURE

1 VOCABULARY: College subjects

A **Match each subject with a possible job description.**

1 architecture	h	a	build machines and bridges
2 biology	____	b	study the way people use money
3 business	____	c	study chemical reactions
4 chemistry	____	d	work in government
5 computer science	____	e	start your own company
6 economics	____	f	take care of sick people
7 education	____	g	study how light and energy work
8 engineering	____	h	design buildings
9 law	____	i	understand the rules of society
10 medicine	____	j	create websites
11 physics	____	k	study living things
12 political science	____	l	help people learn

2 GRAMMAR: Modals of necessity: *have to, need to, must*

A **Circle the correct words to complete the sentences.**

1 I *must* / *didn't have to* take chemistry because I wasn't a chemistry major.
2 I *has to* / *have to* take political science this semester.
3 She *doesn't need to* / *don't need to* take any political science classes.
4 We *needs to* / *need to* sign up for classes today.
5 All students *has to* / *must* choose a major by the spring.
6 I think I want to major in architecture, but I'm not sure. I *need* / *need to* take some classes and see how it goes before I decide.

B **Find the mistakes and write correct questions. Then answer with true information.**

1 Did you had to take the class twice?

Did you have to take the class twice?

No, I didn't have to take it twice. I only had to take it once.

2 Do the rules say that you must to get to class on time?

3 Do I need to taking a business class to get a good job?

4 Is it true that students don't must choose majors at the beginning of the term?

5 Does the teacher has to give a final exam?

6 Do we have to going to class next Monday?

3 GRAMMAR AND VOCABULARY

A **Write answers to the questions. Use *have to, don't have to,* and *must* in your answers.**

1 If you want to work in city government, what kinds of classes do you have to take?

2 Do you know someone who is a science major? What are some of the courses that they don't need to take?

3 Henry wants to design houses. What kinds of classes does he need to take?

4 Alice is taking business classes. What do you think her career goal is?

5 What is your career goal? What kinds of classes do you need to take to succeed in that career?

9.2 HOUSE RULES

1 VOCABULARY: Employment

A Unscramble the letters to make words.

1	eemloyrp	*employer*	7	lyapp	
2	gmnaae		8	ccattonr	
3	eiofoprssn		9	eeettirrmn	
4	aeerrc		10	eihr	
5	wigknor orhsu		11	refi	
6	aweg		12	lsryaa	

B Complete the email with the correct form of the words from exercise 1A. The first letter of each word is given to you.

To: All students
From: President Galarza
Subject: New Work-Readiness Course

The university is now offering a work-readiness course to help any student who is about to graduate and start a new [1] *career* . The course is designed to prepare you for any [2]p ______ – from architect to accountant. Topics cover how to [3]a ______ for a new position, how to make sure you get a fair [4]s ______ or [5]w ______ , and how to successfully [6]m ______ other workers. This course will teach you how to succeed as an employee from the moment you are [7]h ______ until [8]r ______ . Instructors will answer questions about different kinds of [9]e ______ and can offer advice before you sign a [10]c ______ . Please visit the university's homepage to sign up.

2 GRAMMAR: Modals of prohibition and permission

A Put the words in the correct places in the chart. You will use one word twice.

can can't could may may not must not

It is not allowed.	You have permission.	You don't have permission.

B **Complete the sentences with the words in the box. Different answers are possible.**

can	can't	could	may	must not

1 This is the third time you've been late. You can't / must not be late for work again.
2 __________ I take a break now? I need to eat something.
3 You __________ work at home on Friday. I'd like you to be here in person for the meeting.
4 He __________ come to the meeting. He might have some good ideas to share.
5 __________ I work on the project, too? It sounds like fun.

3 GRAMMAR AND VOCABULARY

A **Think of someone you know who can work from home sometimes. Answer the questions.**

1 What is his or her job?
____

2 Who is his or her employer?
____

3 What is his or her salary or hourly wage? If you're not sure, you can guess.
____

4 How often can he or she work from home? Are there times when he or she *can't* work from home?
____
____

5 Does this person find it easy or difficult to manage his or her time? Explain.
____
____

6 What are his or her working hours from home? Can they be different from the hours at his or her usual workplace?
____
____

7 Would you like to have his or her job and the ability to work from home? Why or why not?
____
____

9.3 A NEW CHALLENGE

1 FUNCTIONAL LANGUAGE: Expressing confidence and lack of confidence

A **Match each statement with a response.**

1 That won't be a problem.	____	**a**	Why not?
2 I'm not sure I can handle that.	____	**b**	Great!
3 I don't think I'm strong enough.	____	**c**	Oh, but it's really easy.
4 That doesn't bother me.	____	**d**	I'm glad to hear that.
5 I think I can handle that.	____	**e**	You'll be fine. Don't worry.
6 That concerns me a little.	____	**f**	Then let's start tomorrow.

2 REAL-WORLD STRATEGY: Focusing on reasons

A **Insert the phrase *The thing is* in the correct place in each sentence.**

1 Basketball? I'm not sure I can handle that. ^The thing is, I can't throw very well.

2 Thanks for inviting me, but I can't go. I have to study for a test.

3 I'd love to go, but I have to stay home tonight. I have to take care of my roommate because she's sick.

4 I don't think I'm strong enough. I broke my leg a few months ago. I was skiing with some friends.

5 I don't think I can make it. But thanks for asking. I had to work late last night, and I'm really tired.

3 FUNCTIONAL LANGUAGE AND REAL-WORLD STRATEGY

A **Complete each conversation with a phrase in the box and *The thing is*.**

I don't think I'm strong enough.
I'm not sure I can handle that.
That concerns me a little.

Conversation 1

A Would you like to go skateboarding with me and some of my friends on Saturday?

B No thanks. 1 ___The thing is___, I've never skateboarded before.

A It's easy! And it's fun. We usually skate down that big hill by the park.

B That sounds really scary! 2 ____________

A Oh, I think you can. You should at least try it once.

Conversation 2

A Do you want to go to a yoga class with me?

B 3 ____________

A You don't have to be. It mostly involves stretching.

B Thanks for asking, but I don't think so. 4 ____________, I don't think I'll like it.

Conversation 3

A How long is this hike going to be?

B It's not a long hike – just a couple of miles. And it ends at the top of a mountain! It's beautiful.

A 5 ____________, but I guess it will be OK.

B What are you worried about?

A I'm worried about going to the top of the mountain. 6 ____________, I'm kind of afraid of heights.

9.4 A JOB SEARCH

1 READING

A **Read the job ad for a computer programmer and the two résumés. Then choose the best person for the job.**

The best person for the job is ______________________ .

Responsibilities:
You will help us create computer programs and applications. You will also write reviews of other companies' programs and apps. You can make your own working hours, but you must come into the office in downtown Los Angeles once a week.

Qualifications:
You need to have a four-year degree in computer science. You should have at least two years of work experience. You must have good communication and writing skills and work well with a team.

Katya Petrov

345 Fell Street, Dallas, Texas 75001   415-555-9921   kpetrov77@cup.org

PROFESSIONAL PROFILE

I have a degree in computer science with five years of experience as a computer programmer at an online startup. I wrote articles about technology for my college newspaper, where I worked closely with a group of writers, editors, and photographers.

Elisa Gómez García

1733 J Street, Los Angeles, California 90015   310-555-2910   egomezgarcia@cup.org

PROFESSIONAL PROFILE

I have a degree in computer science with two years of experience creating smartphone apps for a large international company. While I was in college, I was the manager of the computer lab. I worked with a team of five, and I wrote a newsletter for the computer science department.

B READ FOR DETAIL **Identify the information in the profile of the best candidate that makes her the right person for the job.**

1 degree: ______________________
2 experience: ______________________
3 writing skills: ______________________
4 teamwork: ______________________
5 location: ______________________

2 LISTENING

A 9.01 **Listen to Min-kyu talking to Laura about his work experience. Then read the statements and check (✓) *True, False,* or *Not given*. Then listen again and correct the false statements.**

	True	False	Not given
1 Min-kyu has a degree in business.	☐	☑	☐
He has a degree in law.			
2 He was an office assistant in a law office.	☐	☐	☐
3 He organizes schedules in his current job.	☐	☐	☐
4 He wrote computer programs.	☐	☐	☐
5 He studied Korean in college.	☐	☐	☐

3 WRITING

A **Think of someone you know who has an interesting or unusual job. Imagine what information is on that person's résumé. Complete the résumé with information about that person. Use parallel structures in your bulleted lists.**

CONTACT INFORMATION

EXPERIENCE
-
-
-
-
-

SKILLS
-
-

EDUCATION
-
-

CHECK AND REVIEW

Read the statements. Can you do these things?

UNIT 9	Mark the boxes. ☑ I can do it. ? I am not sure. I can …	If you are not sure, go back to these pages in the Student's Book.
VOCABULARY	☐ talk about college subjects. ☐ talk about employment.	page 86 page 88
GRAMMAR	☐ use modals of necessity: *have to, need to, must.* ☐ use modals of prohibition and permission.	page 87 page 89
FUNCTIONAL LANGUAGE	☐ express confidence or lack of confidence. ☐ use *the thing is* to focus on reasons.	page 90 page 91
SKILLS	☐ write the main part of a résumé. ☐ use parallel structures.	page 93 page 93

10.1 GREEN CLOTHES

1 VOCABULARY: Describing materials

A **Check (✓) all of the adjectives that describe each item.**

	Hard	Soft	Natural	Artificial
1 cotton T-shirt	☐	☑	☑	☐
2 glass vase	☐	☐	☐	☐
3 leather wallet	☐	☐	☐	☐
4 metal key	☐	☐	☐	☐
5 plastic bag	☐	☐	☐	☐
6 polyester pants	☐	☐	☐	☐
7 stone wall	☐	☐	☐	☐
8 wood house	☐	☐	☐	☐
9 wool sweater	☐	☐	☐	☐

B **Write two objects that match each description. For each item, choose one object from the box and add one of your own ideas.**

a big box of books	a bookshelf	a pair of thick socks
a pencil	a raincoat	~~a water glass~~

1 fragile: a water glass ______ ______
2 heavy: ______ ______
3 light: ______ ______
4 strong: ______ ______
5 warm: ______ ______
6 waterproof: ______ ______

2 GRAMMAR: Simple present passive

A **Check (✓) the passive sentences. Circle the passive verbs.**

☑ 1 This shirt (is made) of eco-friendly organic cotton.
☐ 2 That color looks great on you.
☐ 3 Does this hat look silly on me?
☐ 4 Jeans are worn by people all over the world.
☐ 5 In most places, shorts aren't sold in the winter.
☐ 6 How many pairs of shoes are sold every day?

B **Complete the sentences with the simple present passive forms of the verbs in the box.**

~~give~~ make sell use wear write

1 Every time someone buys a pair of shoes, another pair ___is given___ to someone who needs them.
2 Who ________ this book ________ by? I can't read the author's name.
3 Plastic ________ in millions of different products, from water bottles to cars.
4 ________ winter coats ________ here?
5 What ________ this sweater ________ of?
6 These days, jeans ________ to formal and informal events.

3 GRAMMAR AND VOCABULARY

A **Make sentences with the phrases and verbs in the chart. Add two of your own ideas. Use the simple present passive forms of the verbs.**

Waterproof materials	make	in the earth
This T-shirt	use	easily
Most boots	break	of cotton
Metal	need	in the winter
Fragile objects	find	in rain boots
A warm coat		of leather
________		________
________		________

1 *Waterproof materials are used in rain boots.*
2 ________
3 ________
4 ________
5 ________
6 ________
7 ________
8 ________

10.2 GLOBAL OR LOCAL?

1 VOCABULARY: Production and distribution

A **Find 12 more vocabulary words in the word search.**

catch	~~deliver~~	design	export	freeze
grow	import	manufacture	pick	produce
ship	store	transport		

D	E	R	T	C	I	S	H	E	N	I	L	O	I	I	R	V
E	D	X	R	X	R	E	W	Y	K	G	W	A	H	M	E	D
X	E	Y	A	U	S	R	W	O	H	P	F	M	U	P	O	C
P	L	O	N	N	P	R	O	D	U	C	E	M	L	O	T	B
A	I	M	S	F	H	A	E	K	R	S	C	J	U	R	I	P
C	V	E	P	A	K	E	X	P	O	R	T	R	I	T	N	L
R	E	A	O	B	X	Y	P	L	W	A	R	G	P	I	C	K
S	R	E	R	A	N	U	G	C	W	Q	P	X	U	C	M	O
T	E	R	T	W	O	L	G	K	S	H	I	P	O	A	S	U
B	S	P	E	X	P	O	R	T	S	T	Y	P	W	T	E	R
C	A	Y	C	R	J	I	O	D	E	U	L	N	M	C	O	Z
Z	R	F	U	N	W	O	W	P	M	C	F	T	S	H	G	P
F	R	H	Z	W	A	O	L	E	F	T	R	Y	N	I	W	Z
G	M	A	N	U	F	A	C	T	U	R	E	T	R	I	V	S
E	X	O	L	P	W	D	T	B	W	C	E	N	O	W	X	R
C	S	T	O	R	E	S	L	O	P	E	Z	R	T	U	B	C
M	E	S	A	Y	W	J	W	E	I	D	E	S	I	G	N	L

2 GRAMMAR: Simple past passive

A **Find the mistakes and write correct sentences.**

1 These flowers was cut yesterday.
These flowers were cut yesterday.

2 The oranges were take to grocery stores.

3 All of the milk were produced in the local area.

4 The coffee was ship from Guatemala.

5 Most of our vegetables grown in California.

6 These herbs was planted last year.

B **Use the words to write sentences or questions in the simple past passive.**

1 these vegetables / grow / on nearby farms / ?
Were these vegetables grown on nearby farms?

2 the rice / not produce / here / .
____

3 the fruit / import / from South America / .
____

4 all of the food / make / by local restaurants / .
____

5 where / these plates / produce / ?
____

3 GRAMMAR AND VOCABULARY

A **Circle the best verb for each sentence. Then complete each sentence with the simple past passive form of the verb.**

1 Too many fish *were caught* last year, so fishing is not allowed this year.
a manufacture **b** grow (**c**) catch

2 This meat ______________, and sometimes the cold temperature changes the taste.
a export **b** pick **c** freeze

3 Where ______________ your cell phone ______________? In China?
a manufacture **b** import **c** grow

4 The package ______________ yesterday. Did you receive it?
a export **b** deliver **c** produce

5 These strawberries are really fresh. They ______________ this morning.
a pick **b** freeze **c** design

10.3 WHAT TO BUY?

1 FUNCTIONAL LANGUAGE: Questioning and approving of someone's choices

A **Circle the best expressions to complete the conversations.**

Conversation 1

A I'm going to order the pizza.

B [1]*Do you really need that?* / *Are you sure you want to get that?* Cheese always gives you a stomachache.

A That's true. OK, I'll get the salmon.

B [2]*Why would you want to buy that?* / *I think you made the right choice.* I'll get the salmon, too!

Conversation 2

A I'm going to buy this Bluetooth speaker.

B [3]*Why would you want to buy that?* / *Now that's a good idea.* It doesn't sound very good.

A I know, but it's shaped like a little bear. It's funny.

B [4]*Do you really need a bad speaker?* / *I think you made the right choice.*

A No, I guess not. I'll put it back.

B [5]*Are you sure you want to get that?* / *That's what I would do.*

2 REAL-WORLD STRATEGY: Changing your mind

A **In each conversation, write the bold expression in the correct place. Write an ✘ where the expression can't go.**

1 **On second thought,**

A I'm going to buy a chicken to cook for dinner.

B That sounds good. ______ How are you going to cook it?

A Maybe I'll roast it. ______ I'm going to make spaghetti. ______ We had chicken last night.

B I love spaghetti. ______ Can I come over for dinner?

A Sure!

2 **Now that I think about it,**

A This looks like a fun game. I'm going to get it.

B I think I played that game at Sam's house.

A Oh, really? ______ I thought it was new.

B ______ It's been out for about a month.

A Oh. ______ I already have it at home! ______ I forgot I had it.

3 FUNCTIONAL LANGUAGE AND REAL-WORLD STRATEGY

A **Complete the conversation with the phrases in the box.**

On second thought	Now that's a good idea.	Why would you want to buy a new one?

A I'm going to buy a new tablet this weekend.
B Don't you already have one?
A Well, I used to have one, but I gave it to my sister.
B That's very generous! Why did you give it to her?
A Because she needed one. And anyway, I didn't really use mine.
B 1 ______________________ You never used your old one!
A That's true. 2 ______________________, maybe I'll save my money.
B 3 ______________________

B **Read the situation about two people. Write a conversation like the one in exercise 3A. Use the phrases in the box.**

Person A wants to buy a jacket. It's too small, but it's on sale.

Person B tries to convince Person A not to buy the jacket.

I think you made the right choice.	Are you sure you want to get that?
Now that I think about it	

A ______________________
B ______________________
A ______________________
B ______________________
A ______________________
B ______________________
A ______________________
B ______________________

10.4 NOT JUST CUSTOMERS – FANS

1 LISTENING

A 10.01 LISTEN FOR DETAIL **Listen to the podcast. Answer the questions.**

1 What kind of company do Jackie and Christopher have?
It's a cookie company.
2 When did they close their company?
3 Why did they start their business again?
4 How is the business different now?
5 Where are their customers?

2 READING

A **Read a customer's feedback about Cookie Bites. Answer the questions.**

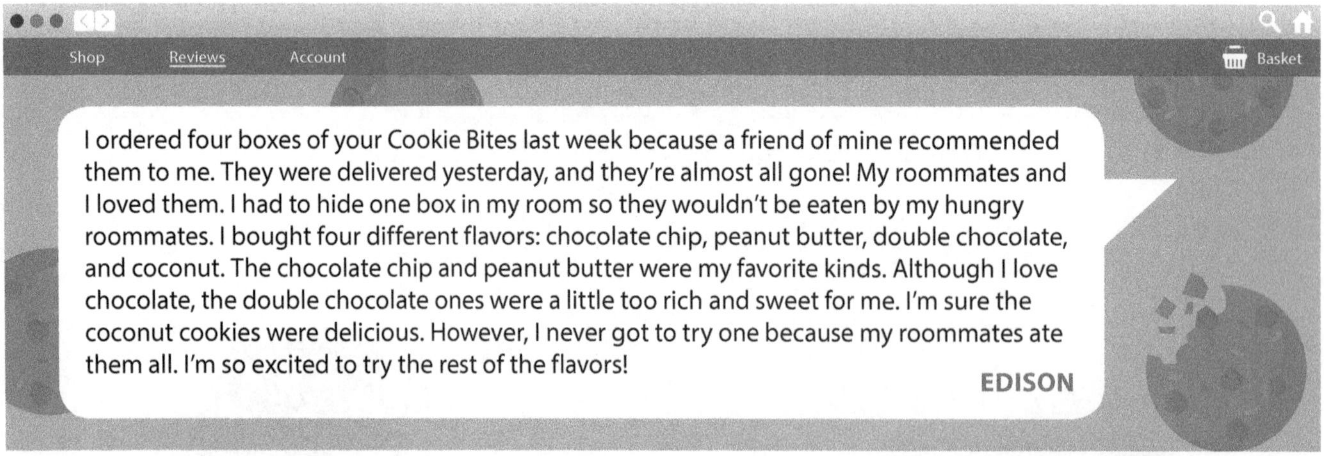

I ordered four boxes of your Cookie Bites last week because a friend of mine recommended them to me. They were delivered yesterday, and they're almost all gone! My roommates and I loved them. I had to hide one box in my room so they wouldn't be eaten by my hungry roommates. I bought four different flavors: chocolate chip, peanut butter, double chocolate, and coconut. The chocolate chip and peanut butter were my favorite kinds. Although I love chocolate, the double chocolate ones were a little too rich and sweet for me. I'm sure the coconut cookies were delicious. However, I never got to try one because my roommates ate them all. I'm so excited to try the rest of the flavors!

EDISON

1 What product is Edison's feedback about?
It's about Cookie Bites.
2 What is his general opinion about the product?
3 Is his feedback all positive, all negative, or a little of both? Explain.
4 Who did he share the product with?
5 Is he going to buy the product again? How do you know?

3 WRITING

A **Think of a product that you use every day and don't really think about, such as toothpaste, dish soap, or shampoo.**

- What is the product?

  ____

- Why do you continue to buy the same product?

  ____

- What do you like about it?

  ____

- What do you dislike about it?

  ____

B **Write a post giving feedback about the product from exercise 3A. Use *however* and *although* to contrast ideas.**

____

____

____

____

____

____

____

____

CHECK AND REVIEW

Read the statements. Can you do these things?

UNIT 10	Mark the boxes. ☑ I can do it. ? I am not sure. **I can …**	If you are not sure, go back to these pages in the Student's Book.
VOCABULARY	☐ **describe materials.**	page 98
	☐ **talk about production and distribution.**	page 100
GRAMMAR	☐ **use the simple present form of the passive.**	page 99
	☐ **use the simple past form of the passive.**	page 101
FUNCTIONAL LANGUAGE	☐ **question or approve of someone's choices.**	page 102
	☐ **use expressions for changing your mind.**	page 103
SKILLS	☐ **write feedback about company products.**	page 105
	☐ **use *however* and *although* to contrast ideas.**	page 105

11.1 SECRETS OF SUCCESS

1 VOCABULARY: Succeeding

A **Complete the sentences with the words in the box and the correct prepositions (*at*, *out*, *over*, or *up*).**

figure get ~~give~~ give keep set stand work work

1 My economics class is really hard, but I don't want to *give up* yet. I know I can do better.
2 If you ______ writing well, you'll get better at it.
3 You're doing a great job. ______ the good work.
4 I don't stay mad. I ______ things quickly.
5 I ______. Learning how to code is too hard. I can't do it.
6 My laptop isn't working, and I can't ______ what's wrong.
7 I want to ______ my own business as soon as I graduate from college.
8 This job opportunity didn't ______, but don't worry. You have three more interviews this month.
9 People ______ at work when they work hard to achieve big goals. Colleagues notice them.

2 GRAMMAR: Phrasal verbs

A **Put each phrasal verb from exercise 1A in the correct place in the chart.**

No object	With object, separable	With object, inseparable
	give up	

B **Use phrasal verbs in the chart to complete the sentences so they are true for you.**

1 I always try my hardest to *speak English with my teacher*. Even though it is difficult sometimes, I never *give up*.
2 I think I've been doing a really good job ______ lately. I hope to ______ it ______ and continue my success.
3 ______ is someone who I think is always the most interesting person in the room. This person almost always ______ in a crowd.
4 I was having trouble finding the answer to a problem in my life recently, but I finally ______ it ______. Now I know I have to ______.

3 GRAMMAR AND VOCABULARY

A **Find the errors in the phrasal verbs. Write correct sentences.**

1 If you don't want to stand it out in a group, don't ask a lot of questions.
If you don't want to stand out in a group, don't ask a lot of questions.

2 I'm going to set my office out today.

3 Your work has been excellent. Keep up it.

4 I'm working out being a better listener because I want to be a good manager.

5 When you fail, it can be hard to get it over.

6 Can you help me figure out it?

7 Don't give it up! You can do it!

B **Answers the questions.**

1 When you work at something for a while and it doesn't work out, what do you do?

2 Have you ever given up and quit a job, a class, a club, or something else? What was it? Why did you give up?

3 How do you get over big disappointments?

4 Do you like to stand out? Why or why not?

11.2 NOW THAT'S INTERESTING!

1 VOCABULARY: Opportunities and risks

A **Circle the correct words to complete the sentences.**

1 Can I borrow your laptop? I need to do some *research / options*.
2 You should carefully *reward / consider* your decision before you decide whether to quit your job.
3 One of my *goals / situations* is to go to college.
4 The *purpose / situation* of this visit is to see if I like the city enough to move there.
5 There are *risks and goals / advantages and disadvantages* to working part-time. One good thing is you have more time for school and family. One bad thing is you don't make as much money as you would with a full-time job.
6 I have a couple of *effects / options*. I can work and save money for a couple of years and then go to school, or I can take out a loan and go to school now.
7 I applied for 30 jobs last month. The *risk / result* was that I got five job offers!
8 I found someone's wallet on the street and sent it to him in the mail. He offered me a $100 *reward / result*!
9 Quitting my job is a big *risk / effect* because it's hard to find a job right now, but I'm really unhappy at work.
10 I can't get a job without a driver's license, but I can't get a driver's license until I have an address here. And I can't pay for a new apartment without a job. It's a strange *purpose / situation*.
11 Traveling to other countries has had a really positive *goal / effect* on my life. It has given me a lot of self-confidence.

2 GRAMMAR: Present and future unreal conditionals

A **Match the sentence halves.**

1 If it were nice outside,	d	a	if her company allowed it.
2 If I had to choose a place to go for dinner,	____	b	if you met her.
3 You would like my friend Sarah	____	c	I would visit my sister more often.
4 I would be happier with my job	____	d	I wouldn't have to wear this big coat.
5 If I had a car,	____	e	he would study architecture.
6 Michael would start his own business	____	f	they would buy a condo by the beach.
7 Cynthia would join the gym nearby	____	g	if he had more startup money.
8 If David went back to school,	____	h	I would pick a Vietnamese restaurant.
9 If Vince and Mary sold their house,	____	i	if the membership weren't so expensive.
10 Michelle would work from home	____	j	if it weren't so far away.

B **Complete each sentence with the correct forms of the verbs in parentheses ( ). Then answer the questions so they are true for you.**

1 **A** If I *owned* (own) a big house, I ______ (ask) my family to live with me. Would you?

B *No, but I think I'd ask all my friends to live with me if I owned a big house!*

2 **A** I ______ (not quit) my job if I ______ (have) a million dollars. What about you?

B ______

3 **A** If my friends ______ (move) far away, I ______ (be) sad. How would you feel?

B ______

4 **A** If your best friend ______ (not work) with you, who ______ you ______ (talk to) all day?

B ______

5 **A** ______ the people you live with ______ (be) happy if you ______ (buy) a huge new TV?

B ______

6 **A** Where ______ you ______ (live) if you ______ (have) the chance to live anywhere?

B ______

7 **A** If you ______ (win) a free trip to a beautiful island, who ______ you ______ (take) with you?

B ______

3 GRAMMAR AND VOCABULARY

A **Complete the sentences with your own ideas.**

1 I would consider moving to a new town or city if ______.

2 I wouldn't mind risking my job if ______.

3 If I were in a scary situation in a strange city, ______.

4 I would have more advantages if ______.

5 If I knew that I would definitely get a good result, ______.

11.3 IT'S NOT WORTH IT

1 FUNCTIONAL LANGUAGE: Asking for agreement and agreeing

A **Complete the conversations with the words in the box.**

agree	~~don't~~	especially	know	mean	point	right

A I've worked for this company for five years, and I've never gotten a raise. I should have gotten one by now, [1] ___*don't*___ you think?

B Yeah, [2] ________ when the company is doing so well.

A That's true. This has been the best five years in the history of the company, [3] ________ ?

B Yes, you're right.

A Everyone who has been here during that time should get a raise, you [4] ________ ?

B Yeah, I would [5] ________ with you. I think we've all helped the company grow over the last five years.

A And our team even came up with *all* of the new product ideas in the last three years.

B Good [6] ________ . We should all ask Lúcio for a raise!

A We should! But I don't think we should do it today.

B Why not?

A Lúcio is in a really bad mood today, and when he's in a bad mood, he says "no" to everything.

B I see what you [7] ________ . Let's do it when he's in a better mood.

2 REAL-WORLD STRATEGY: Softening an opinion

A **Rewrite the opinions. Use *I guess* or *I feel like* to soften them. More than one answer is possible.**

1 The TV is so loud. We should ask him to turn it down.

The TV is so loud. I guess we should ask him to turn it down.

2 I don't see the house. We're going the wrong way.

____

3 It's too late to call Dan. Let's call him tomorrow.

____

4 We've been waiting for a long time. The bus isn't going to come.

____

5 This cake tastes terrible. They used salt instead of sugar.

____

B **Match the scenarios with the opinions.**

1 The movie has started, but Claudio hasn't arrived. ____
2 You went to the address of the florist you used last year, but there's a shoe store there now. ____
3 You had a job interview and you couldn't answer a lot of the questions. ____
4 You were going to fly home today, but you broke your leg, so you have to stay a couple more days. ____
5 Sandra is very unhappy at work, and she complains about it a lot. ____

a "I guess the store went out of business."
b "I feel like she should quit her job."
c "I guess he got stuck in traffic."
d "I guess I have to change my flight."
e "I feel like I'm not going to get the job."

3 FUNCTIONAL LANGUAGE AND REAL-WORLD STRATEGY

A **Complete the conversation using the expressions in the box. Use at least two expressions from each column.**

Don't you think?	Yeah, especially when	I guess
, right?	Yeah, I would agree with you.	I feel like
Don't you agree?	Good point.	
, you know?	I see what you mean.	

A I'm trying to choose between two jobs. One of them is for a law office. It pays really well, but there's no chance for promotion. The other is for an online magazine. It doesn't pay as much, but I could get a promotion and more money eventually.
B *You don't really need a lot of money right now because you're living with your parents. Don't you think?*
A ____
B ____
A ____
B ____
A ____

11.4 OUTSIDE THE COMFORT ZONE

1 READING

A **READ FOR DETAIL** **Read the article. Then answer the questions.**

The Helper Experiment

by Thomas Holley

I recently heard that helping others is a good way to achieve happiness. I wondered if this could be true, so I decided to try it. I came up with an experiment: for one month, I would do at least one nice thing for another person every day. This could be anything from holding a door open to taking care of a sick friend.

On the first day, I saw my elderly neighbor carrying a heavy trash bag to the trash can outside. She was really struggling. I went up to her and asked if I could help her. She gratefully gave me the bag, and we started walking back toward our apartment building. When we got to the front door, she thanked me and invited me into her apartment for a cup of tea. We chatted over our tea for a while, and then I went home. I have to say, I felt great! I felt like I did something important that day and made my neighbor's life a little easier.

Over the next few days, I found myself doing more than one nice thing per day. On my day off the first week, I spent almost the whole day looking for people to help. I wanted to figure out exactly why helping people was making me happy, so I did some research. I found out that there are a number of ways that helping people affects us. For example, helping people can increase our self-esteem and confidence. Doing something nice for another person can also give us a sense of purpose. In addition, when we volunteer on a regular basis, we feel a sense of belonging to a group.

During that month, I think I probably did at least a hundred nice things for others. Since then, I've kept up doing at least one helpful thing per day. If I didn't have to work, I would help people all day long! I've even started volunteering at the hospital. I think everyone should try this experiment. It can make us all happier.

1 What point of view does the writer use? *first person*

2 Why did the writer decide to try the "helper experiment"? __________

3 Who did the writer help first? __________

4 How did the writer feel after the first day of the experiment? __________

5 What are three reasons that helping people makes us happy? __________

2 LISTENING

A 11.01 **Listen to the podcast. Complete the sentences.**

1 The speakers are both __________ .

2 Helping others can have __________ on our brains.

3 It can produce chemicals that __________ .

4 These chemicals make us want to __________ .

5 Helping people can reduce __________ .

3 WRITING

A **Write a personal story about a time when you helped someone, or write a story about a time when someone helped you. Explain what happened and how it made you feel.**

CHECK AND REVIEW

Read the statements. Can you do these things?

UNIT 11	Mark the boxes. ☑ I can do it. ? I am not sure. **I can …**	If you are not sure, go back to these pages in the Student's Book.
VOCABULARY	☐ **talk about succeeding.** ☐ **talk about opportunities and risks.**	page 108 page 110
GRAMMAR	☐ **use phrasal verbs.** ☐ **use future unreal conditionals.**	page 109 page 111
FUNCTIONAL LANGUAGE	☐ **ask for agreement and agree.** ☐ **soften an opinion.**	page 112 page 113
SKILLS	☐ **write a personal story.** ☐ **use *On the one hand* and *On the other hand* to compare opposite ways of thinking.**	page 115 page 115

UNIT 12 LIFE'S LITTLE LESSONS

12.1 IT WAS AN ACCIDENT!

1 VOCABULARY: Describing accidents

A **Match the words with their definitions.**

1 be mad at ___g___ | a not to turn something off
2 blame ______ | b to feel sorry for something you did
3 damage ______ | c to accidently hit something and make it fall
4 destroy ______ | d to cause some harm, like scratches or dents
5 fall out ______ | e not to close something
6 feel bad (about) ______ | f to accidentally drop liquid
7 knock off ______ | g to feel angry with
8 leave on ______ | h to take something out of somewhere
9 leave open ______ | i to think something is someone's fault
10 pick up ______ | j to move something around quickly
11 pull out ______ | k to break so badly that repair is impossible
12 shake ______ | l to lift something with your hands
13 slip ______ | m to suddenly move out of the correct position or place
14 spill ______ | n to drop out of somewhere

B **Circle the correct answers to complete the conversation**

A Who [1]*spilled* / *dropped* water on the floor?
B Sorry, Mom. It was me. I accidentally [2]*fell* / *knocked* a glass [3]*off* / *out* of the table.
A That's OK. I'm not [4]*mad* / *feel bad* at you. Let's clean the water off the floor. I don't want anyone to [5]*slip* / *fall out*.
B Oh, there's broken glass on the floor, too. I'll [6]*pick* / *pull* it [7]*out* / *up*.

2 GRAMMAR: Indefinite pronouns

A **Complete the sentences with the words in parentheses ( ).**

1 (something, somewhere, someone)
I think ______ spilled ______ in the kitchen. It smells funny ______ near the refrigerator.

2 (everywhere, everyone, everything)
______ is broken because ______ is throwing things ______!

3 (anyone, anywhere, anything)
I can't find ______ to read ______. Does ______ have a book I can borrow?

4 (nothing, no one, nowhere)
There's ______ on the stove. I guess ______ cooked dinner, but there's ______ to get good food around here.

B **Complete the conversation with indefinite pronouns.**

A I'm trying to plan Mark's birthday party. I don't know [1] *anyone* who can cook. Do you?

B Yeah, I know [2] ______________ who cooks really well. Actually, you know him, too. It's Tómas. He's coming to the party.

A Oh, great. I didn't know he could cook.

B Yeah, he's really good. I have his email address around here [3] ______________ . I'll need to tell him how much food to make. Do you know how many people are coming to the party?

A No, [4] ______________ has replied to the invitation yet. I guess [5] ______________ is busy studying for finals this week.

B That's too bad. I'll ask Tómas if he'll help us cook anyway. Is there [6] ______________ else I can do right now?

A No, there's really [7] ______________ else we can do until we know how many people are coming.

3 GRAMMAR AND VOCABULARY

A **Answer the questions.**

1 What do you usually do when you're mad at someone?

____

____

2 What would you do if you destroyed something in a friend's home?

____

____

3 Have you ever felt bad about anything? Explain.

____

____

4 What would you do if someone blamed you for something, but you didn't do anything wrong?

____

____

5 Imagine this: You're cooking dinner for friends. Some of the food falls on the kitchen floor after you've cooked it. No one sees this happen, but everyone knows that the food is ready. What would you do?

____

____

12.2 LEARNING UNDERWATER

1 VOCABULARY: Describing extremes

A **Write each word in the correct place in the chart.**

~~boiling~~	enormous	exhausted	freezing	huge	magnificent
miserable	starving	terrific	terrified	thrilled	tiny

Temperatures	Sizes	Emotions/Feelings	Opinions
boiling			

B **Complete the sentences with the correct words from exercise 1A.**

1 I'm ________________ that I got the job! I really wanted it!
2 Don't touch that water! I just turned off the heat and it's still ________________!
3 I have to give a presentation to 500 people tomorrow. I'm ________________!
4 This apartment is ________________. It's so much bigger than my apartment.
5 After work, I had to babysit my niece, and then I worked out at the gym for an hour. I'm ________________!
6 I'm always ________________ by about 11:00 a.m. I guess I should have a bigger breakfast.
7 We just met my friends' new kitten. She's so ________________ that she fits in my hand!
8 It's still snowing and our heater just broke. The house is ________________!

2 GRAMMAR: Reported speech

A **Match the direct speech with the reported speech.**

1 Mike: "I'm on a call with João." __b__
2 Anna: "I'm calling João." ____
3 Mike: "I'm going to call João." ____
4 Anna: "I was on a call with João." ____
5 Mike: "We can call João." ____
6 Anna: "I'll call João." ____

a Anna said she was calling João.
b Mike said he was on a call with João.
c Mike said they could call João.
d Anna said she had been on a call with João.
e Mike said he was going to call João.
f Anna said she would call João.

3 GRAMMAR AND VOCABULARY

A **Complete the conversation with the words in the box.**

exhausted freezing ~~miserable~~ starving terrific

Luna How was your hike on Saturday?

Terry It was [1] miserable ! I hated it.

Luna Oh no, why?

Terry It was [2] ________ , and I didn't have a warm coat on.

Luna That doesn't sound like much fun.

Terry Well, I definitely won't do that hike again. How was your weekend?

Luna It was [3] ________ . I saw a movie and went out to dinner with some friends.

Terry It sounds like you had a lot more fun than I did. I'm [4] ________ . Do you want to go eat something somewhere?

Luna Sorry, I can't. It's late. I'm going to be [5] ________ tomorrow if I don't go to bed soon.

B **Answer the questions with reported speech. Use the information from the conversation in exercise 3A.**

1 How was Terry's hike?
She said ________ .

2 What was the weather like on the hike?
She said ________ .

3 Is Terry going to do that hike again?
She said ________ .

4 What did Luna do over the weekend?
She said ________ .

5 Why does Terry want to get something to eat?
She said ________ .

6 Why doesn't Luna want to get something to eat?
She said ________ .

C **Read the situations. Use reported speech to tell what the people said to you. Add details.**

1 a time a friend was thrilled about some good news
My best friend Marina said she got a big promotion at work.

2 a time when a family member was miserable about some bad news
____

3 a time that someone you know felt terrified
____

4 a time when someone in your class or at your job was exhausted
____

12.3 A HOTEL NIGHTMARE

1 FUNCTIONAL LANGUAGE: Describing, asking about, and guessing feelings

A **Complete the words to make sentences. The first letter of each word is given to you.**

1 You must have been f________________.

2 What a n________________!

3 I bet that made you feel g________________.

4 Actually, I was s________________.

5 How did that make you f________________?

6 I bet that made you feel b________________.

B **Complete the conversations with the sentences in exercise 1A.**

Conversation 1

A I thought you were going to be home yesterday.

B I was, but after I got to the airport, I found out that my flight was canceled! There wasn't another flight until the next day! [1] ________________

A [2] ________________ What did you do?

B I really was. I actually yelled at an airline employee. She told me that they had sent me a couple of emails about it.

A Did you get the emails?

B I remembered that I had gotten some emails from the airline, but I hadn't read them. So I read them and saw that she was right.

A [3] ________________

B Yeah, I felt awful.

Conversation 2

A How was your weekend at the beach?

B Well, Tom crashed the car into a tree right before we were going to leave.

A Oh no! [4] ________________

B Well, at first I felt mad, but it really wasn't Tom's fault. The brakes had stopped working, so he couldn't stop. Then the owners of the house we were renting felt bad for us, so they let us stay there for free while the car was being fixed.

A [5] ________________

B [6] ________________ We thought they didn't like us because they weren't very nice to us over the weekend. I'm glad we were wrong about that!

2 REAL-WORLD STRATEGY: Ending a story

A **Write endings to the stories to show they ended in a good way. Use *After all that* and *In the end*.**

Conversation 1

A I was really sick at the end of last year, and I missed my final exams.

B You must have been so upset!

A Actually, I was disappointed. I studied so hard all semester! But it's OK, ______

______

Conversation 2

A I didn't know my cell phone was in my pocket when I jumped into the pool yesterday.

B Oh no! Was it ruined? I bet you were so annoyed.

A Yeah, I was, at first. But ______

______

Conversation 3

A My train got stuck between stations when I was coming home last night.

B What a nightmare! Were you terrified?

A I was a little scared. ______

______

3 FUNCTIONAL LANGUAGE AND REAL-WORLD STRATEGY

A **Put the conversation in the correct order.**

Mari I bet that made you feel good. ____

Mari So what did you do? ____

Mari You must have been furious! ____

Mari Hey, didn't you go on a long road trip a few months ago? __1__

Jack I was lucky. I ran into an old friend. She loaned me some money. ____

Mari How did that make you feel? Did you feel strange taking the money? ____

Jack Yeah, I did. It was fun at first, but my money and credit cards were stolen. ____

Jack No, I was so happy! To say thanks, I cooked dinner for her. We had so much fun. ____

Jack It did. I couldn't stop smiling. In the end, we talked every day for three months, and now we're going to get married! ____

Jack Actually, I was shocked because I'm always really careful. What a nightmare! ____

12.4 LESSONS LEARNED?

1 LISTENING

A 12.01 LISTEN FOR DETAIL **Listen to the lecture. Then complete the sentences.**

1 We can't change the past, but we can talk to people who have ______.
2 The speaker spoke with people who are ______.
3 She learned that important life lessons are ______.
4 Rose taught her that we need to take time to ______.
5 She said that we need friends who we can call ______.
6 Joe told her that people shouldn't ______.

2 READING

A **Read the anecdote. Answer the questions.**

When I was about 12 years old, I was mad at my best friend Andy because another boy told me that Andy had said mean things about me. I was so upset. Andy asked me what was wrong, but I wouldn't tell him. I wouldn't say anything. After a while, Andy was mad at me, too. We stopped talking to each other. I was miserable and I didn't know what to do. I wanted my best friend back, but I was still angry with him. After a couple of weeks, Andy and I both made new friends and we never talked to each other again.

That was a mistake that I won't make again. As I've gotten older, I've learned that it's important to tell your friends and family why you're mad. You might find out that there's actually no reason to be angry. Or you might discover that they had no idea that they had done something you didn't like. Years later, I found out that the other boy had lied to me. I felt bad that I had destroyed my friendship with my best friend just because I didn't tell him what was bothering me.

1 Why was the writer upset with Andy?

______

2 What did the writer do about his situation with Andy?

______

3 How did the situation affect his friendship with Andy?

______

4 What did the writer later learn about the other boy?

______

5 What life lesson did the writer learn from this situation?

______

3 WRITING

A **Think about a mistake you made in the past that you wouldn't make today. What lesson did you learn? Write an anecdote. Use different expressions to avoid repetition.**

CHECK AND REVIEW

Read the statements. Can you do these things?

UNIT 12	Mark the boxes. ☑ I can do it. ? I am not sure. **I can …**	If you are not sure, go back to these pages in the Student's Book.
VOCABULARY	☐ **describe accidents.** ☐ **describe extremes.**	page 118 page 120
GRAMMAR	☐ **use indefinite pronouns.** ☐ **use reported speech.**	page 119 page 121
FUNCTIONAL LANGUAGE	☐ **describe, ask about, and guess feelings.** ☐ **use *In the end* or *After all that* to end a story.**	page 122 page 123
SKILLS	☐ **write an anecdote about a life lesson.** ☐ **use different expressions to avoid repetition.**	page 125 page 125

1.5 TIME TO SPEAK What makes a leader?

A **Decide if you would or would not like to be a leader – for example, a leader of your school or of your country.**

- Make a list of the good things about being a leader.
- Make a list of the difficult things a leader has to do.
- Decide whether being a leader is mostly good or mostly bad.

B **Make an audio recording about the good and bad things about being a leader. End your recording with your decision about whether it is mostly good or mostly bad to be a leader.**

C **Bring your recording to class and listen to your classmates' recordings. How many of you think being a leader is mostly a good thing? How many of you think it is mostly bad?**

2.5 TIME TO SPEAK Things to bring

A **Imagine that someone has an item that you really want, but they won't take money for it. They will only exchange it for something that is very important to you. Write a description of the thing you will exchange.**

B **Bring your description (and, if possible, your item or a picture of your item) to class. Talk with your classmates, showing your items and sharing your descriptions. Then exchange your description for the description of something that you would like to have.**

3.5 TIME TO SPEAK Secret spots

A **Research secret spots in a city that you have visited or would like to visit.**

- Search for "secret spots in [city]."
- Write down three secret spots that look interesting to you.
- Take notes on where each spot is and what you can do there.
- Print out a map of the city and mark the spots on your map.
- Find out how to get from each spot to the next.
- Write directions from one spot to the next spot to the next.

B **Make a video of yourself giving a presentation about the secret spots. In your video:**

- Show the spots on your map.
- Describe each spot.
- Explain how to get from one spot to the next.

4.5 TIME TO SPEAK Microadventures

A **Think of an idea for a microadventure that you could go on with friends. Go online and research it.**

- Write detailed notes about what the microadventure involves (where it is, how you could get there, what you could do there, how long it would take, and who you could go with).
- Make a list of pros (or benefits) of the microadventure.
- Make a list of cons (or possible problems) of the micraodventure.

B **Invite your class on the microadventure. Use your notes to tell them all about it. How many of your classmates would like to go on your microadventure? What are their reasons for going or not going?**

5.5 TIME TO SPEAK Believe it or not ...

A **Go online and find a surprising story about something that was lost and then found years later. Or, tell a surprising personal lost-and-found story.**

- Take notes on the story.
- Write the story in your own words.
- Add one detail to the story that is made up (it didn't really happen).
- Make an audio recording of your story.

B **Bring your recording to class. Listen to each other's recordings. Guess which detail of each story is made up.**

6.5 TIME TO SPEAK If everyone plants something, ...

A **Go online and research creative ways to save energy or cut down on pollution. Choose one idea to focus on.**

- Take notes on the idea.
- Write three reasons explaining how the idea will help solve a problem.
- Make a poster to illustrate your idea and highlight its benefits.

B **Bring your poster to class and present the idea to your classmates. Ask your classmates to discuss its benefits and possible problems. Then ask them to decide if they want to use the idea.**

7.5 TIME TO SPEAK Changing tastes

A **Think of a movie, TV show, or song that you liked five to ten years ago but don't like anymore.**

- Take notes on why you used to like it. Think of at least three reasons.
- Take notes on why you don't like it anymore. Think of at least three reasons.

B **Make a video of yourself describing your movie, TV show, or song. Explain why you used to like it and why you don't like it now. Share your videos in class. Did anyone have similar reasons why they used to like something? Did anyone have similar reasons why they don't like that thing now?**

8.5 TIME TO SPEAK Building a better life

A **Go online and research two time-saving tips that you haven't read about yet.**

- Take notes on the idea.
- Try each tip for a couple of days.
- Take notes on your experiences with the tips.

B **Make an audio recording. Record yourself explaining the tips and giving a review. Tell whether the tips worked or didn't work for you.**

9.5 TIME TO SPEAK Design your perfect job.

A **Go online and find an advertisement for a job that sounds fun to you.**

- Take notes on the qualifications and requirements. What kind of education and skills do you need to get this job?
- Write a résumé for a person who is qualified for the job.

B **Print out the job ad and present the ad and the résumé to the class. See if your classmates can think of other education or skills to add to the résumé.**

10.5 TIME TO SPEAK Shopping psychology

A **Think of a product people buy because they want to improve themselves or because they feel fear. Go online and find a picture or a commercial for the product.**

- Take notes about the product: What is it? How do people use it?
- How does the picture or commercial show what the product does to improve peoples' lives or make them feel safer? Take notes.

B **Show the picture or commercial for your product to your class. Describe what the product is. Explain how the picture or commercial convinces people to buy it. Do your classmates think the product can really improve peoples' lives or help them feel less fear?**

11.5 TIME TO SPEAK Success stories

A **Think of someone who became successful after appearing on a TV competition. You can find ideas on the Internet.**

- Take notes on the person's life before their success: Where did they live? What did they do? How were they trying to be successful? Why were they having trouble?
- Take notes on the TV competition. What kind of competition was it? What were the rules? What did the winner receive?
- Write a short summary of the person's life and how success changed it.

B **Present your summary to your class. If possible, show a short video clip of the person from their TV competition.**

12.5 TIME TO SPEAK Skillful fun

A **Think of something you had a difficult time learning when you were a child. For example, you might have had trouble figuring out how to tie your shoes, understanding the rules of soccer, or learning how to play an instrument.**

- Take notes on the situation: What were you learning? Why was it difficult? How did you feel about the situation?
- Take notes on how the situation ended: Did you keep trying or did you give up? Why? What did you learn?
- Make a video of yourself describing your experience.

B **Share your video with your class. Explain why you think this was or was not a valuable experience for you. If possible, demonstrate the skill to the class.**

The authors and publishers acknowledge the following sources of copyright material and are grateful for the permissions granted. While every effort has been made, it has not always been possible to identify the sources of all the material used, or to trace all copyright holders. If any omissions are brought to our notice, we will be happy to include the appropriate acknowledgements on reprinting and in the next update to the digital edition, as applicable.

Photographs
Key: B = Below, BR = Below Right, CL = Centre Left, CR = Centre Right, TR = Top Right.

All the photographs are sourced from Getty Images.

p. 2, p. 83: PeopleImages/E+; p. 3: KidStock/Blend Images; p. 4: Leon Bennett/WireImage; p. 5 (BR): andresr/E+; p. 5 (TR): Topic Images Inc./Alloy; p. 6: Maskot; p. 7, p. 71: LeoPatrizi/E+; p. 8: fstop123/E+; p. 9 (CL): J.M.F. Almeida/Moment; p. 9 (CR): Tuul & Bruno Morandi/ Photolibrary; p. 11: delihayat/E+; p. 13: martin-dm/iStock/Getty Images Plus; p. 14: Klaus Vedfelt/DigitalVision; p. 15: carterdayne/E+; p. 16: Hannah Foslien/Getty Images Sport; p. 18: aaaaimages/Moment; p. 19: DarthArt/iStock/Getty Images Plus; p. 20: Images By Tang Ming Tung/DigitalVision; p. 21: Martin Polsson/Maskot; p. 22: kitthanes/ iStock/Getty Images Plus; p. 23: Siri Stafford/DigitalVision; p. 24, p. 54, p. 85: Hero Images; p. 26: Zero Creatives/Cultura; p. 27: Ariel Skelley/ DigitalVision; p. 29: Radius Images; p. 30: Adam Gault/OJO Images; p. 31: Shah Saad/EyeEm; p. 35: Shah Saad/EyeEm; p. 36: Trinette Reed/ Blend Images; p. 37: Andreas Kirsch/EyeEm; p. 38: xavierarnau/E+; p. 39: LightFieldStudios/iStock/Getty Images Plus; p. 41: JLPH/Cultura; p. 42: David Crespo/Moment; p. 44: Dave and Les Jacobs/Blend Images; p. 45 (TR): Jeffrey Coolidge/Corbis/Getty Images Plus; p. 45 (BR): Adrian Weinbrecht/Cultura/Getty Images Plus; p. 47: Dawid Garwol/ EyeEm; p. 48: petrovv/iStock/Getty Images Plus; p. 49: Ashley Cooper/ Corbis Documentary; p. 50: Owen Franken/Corbis Documentary; p. 51: cristianl/E+; p. 52: demaerre/iStock/Getty Images Plus; p. 53: ThorMitty/ iStock/Getty Images Plus; p. 57: Oliver Cleve/Photographer's Choice; p. 58: DragonImages/iStock/Getty Images Plus; p. 59: RoBeDeRo/E+; p. 60, p. 70: Blend Images – Jose Luis Pelaez Inc/Brand X Pictures; p. 61: kupicoo/E+; p. 63: DianaHirsch/iStock/Getty Images Plus; p. 65: White-Plaid/iStock/Getty Images Plus; p. 66: PeopleImages/DigitalVision; p. 67: ImagesBazaar; p 69 (TR): Mike Kemp/Blend Images; p. 69 (B): Ozgur Donmaz/Stockbyte; p. 74: dszc/E+; p. 75: Christina Esselman/ Moment; p. 76: John S Lander/LightRocket; p. 77: Baloncici/iStock/ Getty Images Plus; p. 79: gpointstudio/iStock/Getty Images Plus; p. 80: burwellphotography/E+; p. 84: Caiaimage/Rafal Rodzoch; p. 87: Lumina Images/Blend Images; p. 89: Piotr Marcinski/EyeEm; p. 91: fizkes/iStock/ Getty Images Plus; p. 92: Jason Hosking/Taxi; p. 93: Amaia Arozena & Gotzon Iraola/Moment; p. 95: Martin Barraud/OJO Images; p. 96: Ben Gingell/iStock/Getty Images Plus.

Front cover photography by Alija/E+.

Illustration by Denis Cristo (Sylvie Poggio) p. 55.

Audio production by CityVox, New York.

Corpus
Development of this publication has made use of the Cambridge English Corpus (CEC). The CEC is a multi-billion word collection of contemporary spoken and written English. It includes British English, American English, and other varieties. It also includes the Cambridge Learner Corpus, the world's biggest collection of learner writing, developed in collaboration with Cambridge Assessment. Cambridge University Press uses the CEC to provide evidence about language use that helps to produce better language teaching materials.

Our Evolve authors study the Corpus to see how English is really used, and to identify typical learner mistakes. This information informs the authors' selection of vocabulary, grammar items and Student's Book Corpus features such as the Accuracy Check, Register Check, and Insider English.